ERRATUM

The copy on the cover is misprinted and two alterations should be noted.

1 The final sentence of the opening paragraph beginning 'The book also includes chapters ...' should be deleted.

2 The author's biographical affiliation should read as follows:

Julian Le Grand is Director and Professor of Public Policy in the School for Advanced Urban Studies at the University of Bristol. He is also Co-Director of the Welfare State Programme at the Suntory-Toyota International Centre for Economics and Related Disciplines, London School of Economics. His other books include *The Strategy of Equality* (1982), *Not Only the Poor* (1987), *Privatisation and the Welfare State* (1984), *Market Socialism* (1989) and *The Economics of Social Problems* (3rd Edition, 1991).

EQUITY AND CHOICE

EQUITY AND CHOICE

An Essay in Economics and Applied Philosophy

Julian Le Grand
University of Bristol

HarperCollins *Academic*
An imprint of HarperCollins *Publishers*

© Julian Le Grand , 19 91

Published by
HarperCollins*Academic*
77–85 Fulham Palace Road
Hammersmith
London W6 8JB

10 East 53rd Street
New York, NY 10022
USA

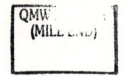

First published in 1991

British Library Cataloguing in Publication Data

Le Grand, Julian
    Equity and choice: An essay in economics and
    applied philosophy.
I. Title
330.1

ISBN 0-04-350065-X
ISBN 0-04-350066-8 pbk

Library of Congress Cataloging in Publication Data

A catalogue record for this book is available from the Library of Congress

Typeset in 11 on 13 point Garamond by M.C.S. Typesetters, Salisbury
and printed in Great Britain by Billings & Sons Ltd.,
Worcester.

To my mother and the memory of my father

Contents

Acknowledgements

This book has been in the making for more years than I care to remember. For much of that time the research was supported in whole or in part by the Welfare State Programme at the Suntory-Toyota International Centre for Economics and Related Disciplines (STICERD) at the London School of Economics. Prior to my employment on the Welfare State Programme, the Nuffield Foundation generously provided me with a research fellowship for a year, during which some of the key ideas were developed. More recently, support has come from the Economic and Social Research Council, under Grant No. X 206 32 2001, and from the School for Advanced Urban Studies at the University of Bristol where I am now based. The assistance of all these organizations is gratefully acknowledged.

Many people have offered comments on parts of the material, most of them so long ago that they have probably forgotten. But I have not, and I would like to express my appreciation here. I owe a particular debt to A. B. Atkinson, who not only has provided many valuable comments on several chapters, but who gave me the opportunity to work with him on the Welfare State Programme in the first place. Without that opportunity, this book would never have been written. Others who have helped with comments and criticisms concerning various aspects of the argument include Nicholas Barr, Brian Barry, John Broome, David Champernowne, Tom Cooley, Frank Cowell, Tony Culyer, Partha

Dasgupta, James Davidson, Jean Dreze, Robert Goodin, Peter Hammond, John Hills, Stephen Jenkins, Mervyn King, Julius Margolis, David Miller, Adam Morton, Joao Pereira, Philip Pettit, Christopher Pissarides, Raymond Plant, Alan Prest, W. B. Reddaway, Andrew Reschovsky, Robert Sugden, Amartya Sen, David Ulph, Albert Weale, Alan Williams and David Winter. Since I have tried to take account of most of what they said, they all have to take some of any credit that may be due to the book; but, of course, none of them is responsible for any errors that remain.

Earlier versions of some of the book's arguments have appeared as journal articles and I would like to thank the publishers and editors of the relevant journals for permission to use the material below. The articles concerned are:

Fiscal equity and central government grants to local authorities. *Economic Journal* (1975), vol. 85, no. 339, pp. 531–47; Reply. *Economic Journal* (1977), vol. 87, no. 348, pp. 780–2.

Equity as an economic objective. *Journal of Applied Philosophy* (1984), vol. 1, no. 1, pp. 39–51.

Optimal taxation, the compensation principle and the measurement of changes in economic welfare. *Journal of Public Economics* (1984), vol. 24, no. 2, pp. 241–7.

Equity, health and health care. *Social Justice Research* (1987), vol. 1, no. 3, pp. 257–74.

Equity, well-being and economic choice. *Journal of Human Resources* (1988), vol. 22, no. 3, pp. 429–80.

Equity versus efficiency: the elusive trade-off. *Ethics* (1990), vol. 10, no. 3, pp. 554–68.

Jane Dickson, Administrative Secretary to the Welfare State Programme, has done much of the typing with her customary efficiency and helpfulness; she has also provided a great deal of other support over the years, more than I can detail here. Prue Hutton and, latterly, Luba Mumford,

Administrative Officers at STICERD, who have made the Centre such an enjoyable and stimulating place to work, deserve much credit. Karen Gardiner did some last minute bibliographical chasing. A succession of editors at what was initially Allen and Unwin, then Unwin Hyman and now HarperCollins, have patiently endured a succession of missed deadlines. Last, but most important, my wife and children have had to put up with the dislocations to family life that, despite all attempts to minimize them, have inevitably taken their toll. To them all, my deepest thanks.

October 1990   Julian Le Grand

1 Introduction

Policy-makers in all societies have values or objectives that inform the making of social judgements and hence guide the making of social decisions. For most societies, these are likely to include attaining an efficient use of scarce resources, and the promotion of an equitable or just distribution of those resources. Other values, too, will affect social decision-making, such as the preservation of individual and collective security and the promotion of individual liberty or freedom.

Properly to take account of all these objectives in the formulation of economic and social policy requires that they be specified in as precise a fashion as possible. Hence, welfare economists and other policy analysts have often found themselves on the terrain of political philosophers in attempting to develop appropriate interpretations of the values involved: interpretations that are both sufficiently general to command a broad consensus and sufficiently specific to permit useful application.

This task has been far from easy. To obtain a consensus on a value-judgement at any other level than the banal is notoriously difficult; to obtain it for an objective that is sufficiently specific to be useful for policy purposes might be considered impossible. Yet some success has been achieved with respect to at least one policy aim: that of efficiency. For several decades there has been a definition that has commanded a wide measure of consensus, at least among economists: that of Pareto-efficiency (or optimality). An allocation of resources is Pareto-efficient if it is impossible to re-allocate those resources in such a way as to make one person better off without making another worse off. This is a proposition of considerable intuitive appeal and one that has been immensely fruitful, forming the entire basis for welfare economics as the latter is conventionally interpreted.

Unfortunately, no comparable consensus has been reached on the appropriate interpretation of the objective that many consider to be at least as important as that of efficiency: that of equity. Although many alternative conceptions have been put forward and extensively discussed, none has achieved a theoretical or practical status comparable to that of Pareto-efficiency. This immediately raises the question as to whether it is possible to define equity in a fashion that both captures the general sense of the term and is useful for policy purposes. Or is such a definition, as some have asserted, a 'mirage': a phantom glimmering on the horizon, apparently desirable and attainable, but whose substance disappears as we approach? It is to these fundamental questions that this book is addressed.

More specifically, the book has a number of aims. The principal one is to evaluate some established (economic) conceptions of equity against specified criteria, and to demonstrate that none performs as well against the criteria as a 'new' conception of economic equity, one that relates the concept to the existence or otherwise of individual choice. A second aim is to illustrate how this concept could be used for analytic and policy purposes, particularly those concerned with various aspects of distribution. Underlying both of these aims is an attempt to demonstrate that equity is not a mirage; that it is possible to derive and to use conceptions of equity that, whatever their merits or demerits, have intellectual substance, and that have at least as much analytic potential as conceptions of other social objectives, such as efficiency or liberty.

The book is written by an economist with philosophical

pretensions and as such is perhaps a little different from the works of some other writers in the area, both political philosophers and economists. With some notable exceptions, political philosophers have commonly focused on the philosophical justification for different interpretations of the concept, while paying little attention to policy application. And with even fewer exceptions (at least in recent years), economists who have addressed equity issues have spent little time on the philosophical or other justification for the particular definition with which they may be dealing, preferring instead to concentrate on deriving results concerning the implications of that definition for resource allocation. While in each case this can be defended on the grounds that this is where their comparative advantage lies, it can at times make for a striking imbalance between, in the case of the philosophers, the depth of the philosophical argument and the cursory treatment of its practical implications, and, in the case of the economists, the sophistication of the economic analysis and the shallowness of its philosophical base. Any attempt to remedy these imbalances by trying to link philosophical argument with economic analysis obviously runs the risk of creating a product that satisfies neither camp. It nonetheless seems important to try, if only to stimulate others to do better.

Inevitably, given the training of its author, the book reflects the biases of economics. However, it is hoped that it will be of interest not only to economists, but also to political philosophers, to social policy specialists and indeed to anyone with an involvement in the analysis of ethics, economics and public policy. Accordingly, in order to make the book as accessible to as wide an audience as possible, the arguments are generally presented in a way that should be understandable to those with little specialized knowledge of economics, with the issues that require more technical treatment in most cases being confined to appendices. The only area where this proved impossible was the material for

Chapter 9; but this chapter may be omitted without serious interruption in the flow of the argument.

The book falls into two parts. The first part (Chapters 2–6) discusses some of the basic theoretical issues. Chapter 2 undertakes some ground-clearing work concerning terminology, examining the relationships between equity and its virtual synonyms, justice and fairness, and between equity and its near homonym, equality. It then discusses the motivation for the whole enterprise, concentrating upon the arguments of those who claim that the search for useful conceptions of equity is a futile one, and therefore that equity should not be included in the list of social and economic objectives that guide policy-making or other social judgements. The conclusion is reached that none of the arguments concerned is sustainable and hence that it is both possible and sensible to attempt to establish an interpretation of equity that will be useful for analytic and policy purposes. However, this does not imply that equity should dominate all other considerations in formulating economic and social policy; the achievement of a fully equitable society may be too expensive in terms of other objectives, and some kind of trade-off may be necessary.

The idea of a trade-off between social values or objectives may be new to some readers; it is discussed further in Chapter 3 in the context of an examination of the supposed trade-off between equity and efficiency. A major purpose of this chapter is to demonstrate that definitions of efficiency can be as problematic as definitions of equity. This includes the definition of efficiency known as Pareto-optimality, which, it is argued, is not really a definition of efficiency at all; rather it incorporates a particular interpretation of social welfare, including a rather curious notion of equity.

Chapters 4, 5 and 6 form the core of the book. Chapter 4 discusses different methods of approach for evaluating conceptions of equity and specifies the approach used in the subsequent chapters. Chapter 5 applies the approach to some of the definitions of equity that have attracted attention in the economics literature and elsewhere; it argues that none of them succeeds in meeting the relevant criteria.

Chapter 6 puts forward an alternative conception: one that relates equity to the existence or otherwise of individual choice. It is argued that this comes more closely than any of the others considered to capturing the essence of the term and to meeting the appropriate criteria.

The aim of the second part of the book (Chapters 7–9) is to show how some of the ideas developed in the first part can be applied to a variety of policy contexts. It is not necessary fully to accept the arguments in the first part of the book to assess the ideas of the second, some of which I hope are worthy of discussion in their own right.

Three problems are analysed, at different levels of theoretical complexity; the distribution of health and health care (Chapter 7), the allocation of intergovernmental grants (Chapter 8) and the measurement of income for tax purposes (Chapter 9). All of these raise important equity issues; other than that, they have little in common. This is deliberate: the intention is to illustrate the applicability of this kind of analysis across a wide range of different problems.

These chapters are of increasing levels of technicality. Chapter 7 should be readily accessible to all readers. Chapter 8 requires some facility with algebra, but should be otherwise unproblematic for non-specialists. Chapter 9, however, deals with issues (particularly those involving non-linear budget constraints) that can only properly be handled with the help of some technical economic apparatus. The book closes with a brief concluding chapter (10).

Finally, having said what I am trying to do in the book, I should perhaps make clear what I am not. In particular, the book is not, and, given the volume of the relevant literature, could not hope to be, a complete review of everything that has been written on equity. This means that I have not always done justice, so to speak, to many major contributions to this literature; an omission for which I can only plead the exigencies of time and space. In particular, the recent revival of interest among economists, political philosophers and others in the question of distributional principles has spawned a number of important works, including those of A. B. Atkinson (1983c), Brian Barry (1989a, 1989b), John Broome (forthcoming), Partha Dasgupta (1982, 1989), Robert Goodin (1985, 1988), David Miller (1976), Philip Pettit (1980), Raymond Plant (1984; Plant, Lesser and Taylor-Gooby, 1980; Hoover and Plant, 1989), Amartya Sen (1973, 1982, 1985), Robert Sugden (1986) and Albert Weale (1978, 1983). Although many of these authors are referred to in what follows, their ideas have often had a broader influence on the material, in a way that makes it difficult to credit them properly in each case. The least I can do is to acknowledge my debt to them here; I can only hope that others will profit from this work as much as I have from theirs.

2 Some preliminaries

There are two issues that it is important to clear out of the way before proceeding. First, there is a question of terminology. Equity is often confused with, or used synonymously with, a variety of other concepts such as fairness, justice and equality. To try to provide a definitive account of all aspects of the relationships between them would be a diversion from the main argument of the book, but it is necessary to delineate as precisely as possible the form that these relationships will take in the discussion.

Secondly, and of more importance, is the motivation for the whole enterprise. Some might feel that the search for acceptable definitions of equity is in fact a futile one; that equity has no place on the list of objectives of economic and social organization; that it should not guide social judgements or be part of the concerns of policy-makers or their advisers. Others would find such a position absurd; for them, the attainment of an equitable distribution of resources is an aim whose position in the list of objectives is at least on a par with others such as the promotion of economic efficiency or the preservation of individual liberty, and perhaps, in some situations, above them. Naturally, the writer of a book primarily concerned with equity is likely to believe that the claims of the second camp are stronger than the first. Nonetheless, there are respectable arguments against including considerations of equity or justice among the values that guide policy, and these need to be addressed.

Equity, justice and fairness

Equity is often used synonymously, or virtually so, with justice and fairness. This is apparent from dictionary definitions of the term. The *Shorter Oxford Dictionary* includes both fairness and justice as part of its definition of equity.[1] It also gives equitable as one of the meanings of fair; and it notes that the word justice is derived from the Latin *justica*, which is translated as 'righteousness, equity'. *Webster's Third New International Dictionary* gives fairness as one of the meanings of equity and includes justice twice as part of its explication of the term.[2] Similarly, just and equitable are given as synonyms of fair (although fair is described as the 'most general of the terms', with just as the least general) and equitable is given as one of the meanings of just.

It would thus appear that, at least to dictionary compilers, equity, fairness and justice are close to being synonyms. This would also seem to be the case in common usage, particularly in regard to economic matters. It is difficult to find phrases incorporating the terms equity or equitable where their replacement by fairness or fair, or by justice or just, would significantly alter the sense of the phrase. For instance, the idea of an 'equitable' distribution of income seems to have broadly the same meaning as a 'fair' or 'just' distribution of income; 'equity' in taxation, the same as 'fairness' or 'justice' in taxation; 'equitable' prices the same as 'fair' or 'just' prices.

However, they are not always used synonymously in the academic literature. In political philosophy, for instance, the term justice in particular seems to have acquired a rather broader meaning. Rawls, in his seminal work on the topic (1972), uses the phrase 'theories of justice' to encompass not only his own two basic principles, which deal with questions of liberty as well as with more conventional notions of justice, but also utilitarian ones. Many authors have followed him; Pettit, for example, entitles his review of recent developments in political philosophy *Judging Justice* (1980), and includes not only Rawls's principles and utilitarianism as theories of justice, but also libertarian principles such as those of Nozick (1974).[3]

However, to use justice in this all encompassing fashion seems a little misleading. For utilitarianism, the aim of 'the greatest happiness of the greatest number' (however that is interpreted) dominates all other possible objectives. Indeed in its purest form there are no other aims; everything is judged according to its contribution to the utilitarian end. For libertarians, the right of individuals not to be (intentionally) coerced by other individuals similarly dominates all other ends; and, for Rawls, his two principles dominate any other principle. In other words, for all three schools of thought, the particular principle or principles to which they adhere are lexicographic: that is, there is no other principle, movement towards the attainment of which would be justified, however great, if it required movement away from attaining the principle concerned, however small. To describe these principles as principles of justice is therefore to define justice as synonymous with 'best' or 'most desirable'. A just distribution or allocation is, under this interpretation, the *optimum optimorum*, or the allocation that is '*right*, all things considered' (Feinberg 1975, p. 108; emphasis in original).

There does not seem to be a great deal of benefit in this identification of justice with 'best', thus conflating a variety of different aims under the umbrella of 'justice'. Utilitarian or libertarian considerations are rather different from considerations of justice as the term is used outside this literature, and it is confusing, to say the least, to proceed as if they were. The confusion is compounded in some of the relevant literature by the use of justice in this over-arching sense simultaneously with the narrower sense of being synonymous, or close to synonymous, with equity. Since there is a range of other expressions to describe situations to which the broader usage has been applied ('best', 'most desirable', 'right, all things considered', 'optimal', 'optimum optimorum'), it seems preferable to confine the term justice to its more conventional interpretation: that is, where it is (virtually) synonymous with equity.

Political philosophers seem rarely to use the term equity; when they do they class it as a 'desert'-based notion of justice (see, for instance, Miller 1976, pp. 333–4). Here they are following social psychologists such as Homans (1961), Adams (1963, 1965) and Sampson (1969), who have developed what is termed 'equity theory' specifically in terms of what people deserve to receive. Some of these views are discussed in Chapter 4 but it is worth noting here that even writers in this tradition tend to use the term as virtually synonymous with justice: for instance, Sampson's definition of equity includes the statement that 'a condition of *justice* obtains when the person gets what they deserve' (p. 259, emphasis added).

Economists have in general tended to use the term equity synonymously with fairness or justice. However, an exception is the 'equity as envy-freeness' school of thought (exemplified by Varian 1974, 1975), the merits of which are discussed in Chapter 5. These writers define 'equitable' allocations as those that are envy-free, and define as 'fair' allocations that are simultaneously envy-free and Pareto-efficient. As with the political philosophers' broader use of justice, this appropriation of the term fairness has little sanction in common usage and seems as likely to cause confusion as to promote clarity. As with 'just' allocations, it seems preferable to identify 'fair' allocations with equitable allocations, and to use terms like 'optimal' or 'best' to describe allocations that satisfy multiple criteria.

As will become apparent in subsequent chapters, I have some sympathy with the social psychologists' view that equity is primarily a desert-based conception; indeed, this may be the key to the distinction between it and broader conceptions of justice. However, to confine the term simply to notions of desert is premature at this stage. Hence, in what follows, particularly when discussing different conceptions of equity, I shall not distinguish between conceptions where the terminology used is that of justice or fairness and those where the terminology is one of equity. Generally, therefore, I shall follow common usage and treat equity, justice and fairness as synonyms.

Equity and equality

Debates on distributional issues are often confused by a failure properly to distinguish between equity and equality. This has generally been to the detriment of proponents of redistribution; for it is easier for their opponents to marshall arguments against the proposition that, say, the distributions should be *equal* than against the proposition that it should be *equitable* (for examples of this setting up of the 'equality' straw man as a target, see Joseph and Sumption, 1979, and the collection of anti-egalitarian essays in Letwin, 1983).

But the two concepts are in fact quite distinct. Equality has a descriptive component, whereas equity is a purely normative concept. Partly as a consequence, equality does not necessarily imply equity, or equity equality. Equality of various kinds may be advocated for reasons other than equity; equitable outcomes may be quite inegalitarian.

As a simple illustration of the relevant points, consider the following example. Suppose a cake is divided between four children according to the percentage distribution [40, 30, 20, 10]. The distribution is clearly unequal, and, if there were no other information, it might also be considered inequitable. But suppose we are then told that the reason for the disparity is that the children are being rewarded in proportion to their contribution to a local fund-raising exercise for charity. Then we might judge the current distribution, unequal though it is, as equitable. Inequality does not, in this case, necessarily imply inequity.

A more subtle example of the confusion that can arise can
be found in the literature concerning the measurement of
inequality. Since Atkinson's path-breaking article on inequality measurement (1970) it has been generally accepted
that the use of statistical measures of inequality, such as the
Gini coefficient or the coefficient of variation, implies the
acceptance of certain values. From this the inference has
been drawn that inequality (and therefore equality) is itself
normative.

But this inference is illegitimate. Measures of inequality
are summary statistics: that is, they compress the (often considerable) amount of information concerning a distribution
into one number, a number that gives an indication of the
dispersion of that distribution. In doing so, they inevitably
emphasize some of the information while suppressing, or
even ignoring altogether, the rest. The choice of summary
statistic thus involves evaluation of the relative merits of the
information emphasized and that suppressed; and this
indeed requires some normative assessment. However, the
fact that the choice of summary measures of inequality
involves value-judgements of this kind does not imply that
the concept itself is normative. It is the emphasis/suppression
of information that creates the necessity for value-
judgements, not the concepts of equality or inequality themselves.

This could be challenged. Return to the example of distributing the cake and consider another way of dividing it
between the four children, that is [35, 35, 25, 5]. Is this
more or less equal than the first distribution [40, 30, 20,
10]? The answer will presumably depend on whether a
transfer of an amount equivalent to five percentage points
from the 'richest' child in the first distribution to the second
richest outweighs in some sense the transfer of five percentage points from the poorest child to the second poorest: and
this can only be resolved by making a value-judgement. But
again this is a measurement issue; one that in this case arises

from the poverty of language. When making the judgement that one distribution is more or less equal than another, several different pieces of information have to be compressed into one dimension so that the assessment of 'more' or 'less' equality can be made. Inevitably, in that process of compression, value judgements have to be made concerning the relative values of the information suppressed or emphasized; value is entering, but only in the process of compression. There is no necessary implication that the concept of equality itself embodies values.

Finally, a further illustration of the separateness of equality and equity is the fact that equality may be advocated for reasons quite unconnected with equity. That most celebrated of egalitarians, R. H. Tawney, argues that equality is desirable because it is a necessary condition for community.

> What a community requires ... is a common culture, because, without it, it is not a community at all. But a common culture ... is incompatible with sharp contrasts between the economic standards and educated opportunities of different classes ... It involves, in short, a large measure of economic equality ... (Tawney 1964, p. 43)

This point is also argued by Atkinson (1983a). Tawney (1964) also argues that equality is desirable because it is conducive to certain kinds of liberty (p. 164 ff); so does Plant (1984). In short, it is possible to be an egalitarian without being necessarily an 'equitarian': a fact which provides further evidence of the distinctness of the two concepts.

Should equity be an objective?

Several economists and philosophers, usually of a libertarian persuasion, have argued that equity should not be included among the objectives of economic organization. There are four reasons for this, which they emphasize to different degrees: impracticality, inappropriateness, immorality and illusion. To include equity among the list of objectives is impractical because agreement on the definition of equity is impossible: individual views on the matter are so diverse that the consensus necessary for the concept to be useful for policy or other purposes can never be achieved. It is inappropriate because equity is value-laden. Unlike, for instance, efficiency considerations, matters of equity involve value-judgements and hence are not amenable to positive analysis. It is immoral because the concern for equity stems from the base emotions, particularly that of envy. And it is illusory because equity is literally a nonsense: a meaningless concept that only masquerades as having content.

The charge of *impracticality* has been levied by, among others, Hayek and Gray. Thus Gray argues: 'It defies experience to suppose that any consensus on relative merits can be reached in a society so culturally diverse (and for that reason so free) as ours ... One of the chief functions of the contemporary ideology of social justice may be ... to generate an illusion of moral agreement, where in fact there are profound divergencies of values' (Gray 1984, pp. 181–2).

However, it is not clear why, among the many possible candidates for common values or objectives, equity or justice should be singled out for this criticism. The meaning of liberty is also open to a wide variety of possible interpretations, as the ongoing debate between the proponents of positive and negative liberty illustrate; the meaning of efficiency is far from uncontroversial, as will be demonstrated at length in the next chapter. Moreover, much of the rest of this book is an argument that there is a core of consistency in many of the ways that the term equity is used; it is for the reader to assess whether that argument is plausible, or whether there remain profound and disabling 'divergencies of values'.

The dichotomy between equity and efficiency implied by the *inappropriateness* argument is misleading. As argued in the next chapter, the definition of efficiency most commonly used by economists (that of Pareto) is not value-free; indeed, it actually incorporates a specific conception of equity. Moreover, it would not be possible to find a definition of efficiency that was value-free; for efficiency can only be defined in relation to more fundamental objectives, acceptance of which is dictated by values. Again, this argument is developed further in Chapter 3.

Yet more generally, positive analysis is not inappropriate simply because value judgements are present. If an agreed definition of equity can be found, then positive analysis can be employed to determine whether a given allocation of resources is or is not equitable according to the definition; just as, with an agreed definition of what constitutes efficiency, positive analysis can be employed to determine whether a given resource allocation is efficient. The problem lies in a lack of agreement concerning the definition of equity, not in an alleged inapplicability of positive analysis.

The argument that the inclusion of equity is *immoral* is derived from the assertion that it stems from an unworthy motivation: that of envy. This view is so widespread among the opponents of attempts to promote equity or justice that it does not need extensive documentation (to pick just one example, see Bauer, 1982, 1983). But ubiquity does not confer legitimacy. There are two main weaknesses with the argument. First, it seems to be factually incorrect. There are many reasons why people subscribe to the cause of equity or justice. Doubtless for some, these include envy; but the commitment may also derive from more sophisticated views of self-interest, including the fear of suffering an injustice, even if none is currently being experienced, or the belief that the more equitable a society, the more stable it is and hence the more desirable a place it is in which to live. Alternatively, the concern for equity may not stem from self-interest at all but from a genuine empathy with the plight of others: an altruistic concern that others, as well as oneself, receive what they ought to receive.

With respect to this last point, it is worth noting that the concern for equity is often allied to the concern for charity (see, for example, Tullock 1983, ch. 1). However, it should also be noted that this is not the same as saying that a concern for equity or justice is identical to charitable or altruistic motivations. The claims of charity are different from the claims of equity.[4] Indeed, as Sidgwick (1907, p. 242) argues 'benevolence begins where justice ends', or as the traditional proverb has it, 'be just before you are generous'. Although the priority of justice over charity implicit in these statements could be challenged (see, for example, Goodin 1985, pp. 16–17), that there is a difference between the two seems undeniable. A gift is charitable if it is given to those who have already been treated equitably; if they had not been so treated, then the gift would not be charitable, but would merely provide them with what is their 'due'.

The second weakness of the envy argument for omitting equity from the list of social and economic concerns is that, *even if* the motivation for some people being concerned about equity is envy, this does not invalidate the concern itself. It will still be necessary for policy prescriptions to attempt to take account of people's concern for equity, regardless of its source, so long as such a concern exists at a significant level. *Ad hominem* attribution of the motivations of those putting forward particular points of view do not in and of themselves invalidate that view or render it irrelevant.

The prime exponent of the argument that equity is an *illusion* is Hayek, in a book appropriately, if provocatively, titled *The Mirage of Social Justice* (1978). Hayek argues that the concept of equity (which he terms social justice) is inapplicable to the outcomes of a spontaneous process such as a free market. No one individual is responsible for a market-determined allocation of resources; no one has decided that each individual should have such-and-such a level of income or such-and-such a level of wealth. Instead, the amounts of income or wealth accruing to each individual are determined by the interaction of the desires, activities and constraints of perhaps thousands of other individuals, mediated through the market mechanisms. In that case, it is impossible to describe market outcomes as just or unjust, equitable or inequitable; it would be like describing as unfair the fact that one area was wet while another was sunny. Any such judgements do 'not belong to the category of error but that of nonsense' (p. 78).

However, this is not an argument against applying equity judgements in contemporary societies. Even if we accept the basic proposition that the outcomes of spontaneous processes cannot be judged in equity terms (and we might not; for instance, if this were correct, then it would imply that the phrase 'life is unfair' is completely devoid of meaning, which does not seem consistent with general usage), it seems quite implausible to suppose that the allocation of resources in mixed economies is a 'spontaneous process'. There is substantial government intervention in the distribution of income and wealth; and government production and/or subsidization of key commodities (such as education, health care, housing and transport) is widespread. Indeed, the very fact that the market is not allowed to allocate resources in some areas suggests that the continued operation of unfettered markets in others is itself the result of human decision. Since Hayek admits (p. 69) that the concept of equity does have meaning when applied to non-spontaneous processes, it would seem that the search for a definition applicable in most societies is not a 'nonsense'. Although the object may be elusive, it is not an illusion.

Conclusion: equity and other objectives

The arguments that the search for a useful conception of

equity is futile, and indeed that the aim should not even appear on the list of social and economic objectives, are unconvincing. It therefore seems reasonable to attempt to find such a conception, and that will be the task of subsequent chapters. However, one question is left unresolved: the relationship of equity or justice to other social values, or, put another way, its ranking on the list of aims or objectives.

Some would argue that it should be at the top. In the often quoted opening to his book, Rawls (1972) asserts that 'justice is the first virtue of social institutions' (p. 1). But he was not the first to do so. The Emperor Ferdinand I pronounced 'Fiat justitia et pereat mundus' (Let justice be done, though the world perish); and William Watson said 'fiat justitia et ruant coeli' (Let justice be done though the heavens fall).[5] Edmund Burke went perhaps the furthest of all when he said 'There is but one law for all, namely, that law which governs all law, the law of our Creator, the law of humanity, justice, equity – the law of nature and of nations'.[6]

However, despite its distinguished parentage, this is not a view shared by the author. The fact that equity is an important consideration in assessing the overall desirability of a particular distribution or allocation does not necessarily imply that it is the *only* consideration, or even that it is the most important. No claim is made here that equity should be ordered lexicographically among social objectives. Rather the allocation of resources, which represents the *optimum optimorum* or 'the best, all things considered', will be the result of trading-off the degree of equity achieved with the degree of achievement of other objectives, such as liberty. But specifying the *optimum optimorum* cannot be done until the objectives to be traded-off are themselves specified and defined; and it is to this prior task, with respect to equity, that much of the rest of this book is addressed.

However, before that task is undertaken, the notion of a trade-off between objectives – a notion that may be alien to some readers – needs further discussion. The next chapter develops the idea in the context of the well-known, but ill-defined, trade-off between equity and efficiency.

Notes: Chapter 2

1 The first three meanings given in the 1977 edition of the *Shorter Oxford Dictionary* are : i The quality of being even or fair; impartiality, even-handed dealing. ii That which is fair or right. iii The recourse to general principles of justice to correct or supplement the ordinary law. The remaining meanings concern jurisprudential and financial meanings of the term.

2 The entry in *Webster* includes: a free and reasonable conformity to accepted standards of natural right, law and justice without prejudice, favoritism or fraud and without rigor entailing undue hardship : justice according to natural law or right; fairness.

3 The tradition perhaps stems from Aristotle himself, for whom, as Miller (1976, p. 17) notes, justice was equivalent to virtue in general. Miller goes on to say that 'we are perhaps fortunate that we have lost' this sense of the term; this is a little optimistic, as the discussion in the main text indicates.

4 For an important discussion of altruism and its implications for economics, see Collard (1978).

5 I am grateful to Michael Lockwood for these quotations.

6 Speech on 28 May 1794.

3 Equity versus efficiency: the elusive trade-off

It is commonly asserted that there is, or that in most situations there is likely to be, a trade-off between equity and efficiency. That is, the implementation of a policy measure designed to 'increase' one may result in a 'decrease' in the other. For example, a social security system that reduces poverty, thus promoting greater equity under most interpretations of that term, may also reduce individuals' incentives to work or to save, thus creating inefficiency – at least under some interpretations of that term. Another example might be selective education, accused by some of being ultimately incompatible with equality of educational opportunity and thus with equity, but advocated by others as promoting 'excellence', and hence efficiency. Yet another case might be a health care programme on the dangers of smoking that increased the average life-expectancy of all groups in the population, thus promoting efficiency, but produced a greater increase in life-expectancy for the better-off (who, for various reasons, were more responsive to the message) than for the poor, thus increasing the gap between these groups and arguably increasing inequity.

There are several questions that can be asked about this trade-off. Some of them are empirical. Does social security really discourage people from working? Does selective education actually produce better exam results on average than more universal systems? Do anti-smoking campaigns have a greater impact on the better-off than on the poor? And so on. These are important and controversial questions; but they are not my concern here. Rather, I intend to concentrate on the theoretical issues concerning the intrinsic nature of the equity–efficiency trade-off. In particular, I want to examine the question of whether the general notion of a trade-off between the two actually makes sense. A necessary condition for it to do so is that efficiency is a social and economic objective in the same sense that equity is an objective. But does efficiency have the same status as equity, or indeed as other possible objectives of economic and social organization, such as liberty? If it does not, and it will be one of the contentions of this chapter that at least in one important sense it does not, then what do people mean when they talk of the equity–efficiency trade-off?

The chapter begins with a distinction between two kinds of trade-off, either of which could form the basis for 'the' equity–efficiency trade-off. There follows a discussion of various possible interpretations of the term efficiency, and their implications for the existence or otherwise of the trade-off. There is a brief concluding section. A more technical exposition of some of the arguments can be found in Appendix 3.1 (p. 35).

Types of trade-off

The first point to be made is that there are two different kinds of phenomenon to which the phrase equity–efficiency trade-off could refer. The first concerns values, the second what might be termed production.

The ideas underlying the value trade-off were first laid out systematically by Barry (1965). He argued that, when evaluating social outcomes, it was not necessary for rationality in that evaluation to assume that reaching one objective should always dominate reaching another. Rather, the 'extent' to which one objective was attained could be traded off, or substituted for, the extent to which another was attained. In the equity–efficiency context (the example discussed by Barry) it would be perfectly consistent with most notions of rationality for someone to consider an allocation of resources that was highly efficient but grossly inequitable as equally good (or equally bad) as one that was extremely equitable but highly inefficient. 'The fundamental idea ... is that although two principles need not be reducible to a single one, they may normally be expected to be to some extent substitutable for one another. The problem of someone making an evaluation can thus be regarded as the problem of deciding what mixture of principles more or less implemented out of all the mixtures which are available would be, in his own opinion, best'.

In passing, it should be noted that, as Barry points out (1965, p. 6), any reference to the 'extent' to which an objective can be attained contains within it the assumption that movement towards the objective can be measured or quantified in some way. In making this assumption (as is done throughout this chapter), it is not intended necessarily to imply that meaningful numbers can be constructed that represent the level of efficiency or equity that characterizes a particular allocation of resources. All that is necessary for the discussion is that it is meaningful to say that one outcome is more equitable, or more efficient than another: an ordinal, rather than a cardinal, requirement.

The idea that in making social evaluations people might be indifferent between various combinations of objectives or principles, just as in making their consumption decisions they might be indifferent between various combinations of goods, seems reasonable. Moreover, it is a way of resolving dilemmas concerning apparent inconsistencies in people's moral decisions that have puzzled some economists. For instance, Friedman (1962, p. 165) gives two examples of the trade-off between equity and liberty that he thinks provokes inconsistent reactions. One is where three individuals are starving and a fourth has food but refuses to give it to them; the other is where four people are walking down the street, one finds a ten dollar note in the gutter and refuses to share it with the others. Friedman thinks that a common judgement would be that the three 'poorer' individuals in the first case would be justified in overriding the liberty of the fourth and forcing a more equitable distribution, but that the individuals in the similar position in the second case would not be justified in doing so: a reaction that he would consider inconsistent. But what the examples show is that people may be prepared to trade-off 'more' liberty to promote 'more' equity if the initial situation is already grossly inequitable (as in the first case) than if it is already broadly equitable (as in the second case): a position that seems quite consistent with commitment to both values.

So the idea of a trade-off in terms of social values or objectives does not seem unreasonable. However, whatever the plausibility of the idea, it is not likely that, when people refer to the equity–efficiency trade-off, it is substitutability in terms of values that they have in mind. Rather, they may be concerned with what might be termed 'production-substitutability': that is, with the ability of a policy measure or of other aspects of the economic and social system to *deliver* different combinations of objectives. The sort of questions involved here are not value in nature, but are empirical; they concern the possibility or feasibility of alternatives. Is it possible or feasible to allocate resources within the economy in a way that is both 'fully' equitable and 'fully' efficient? If not, then what are the various combinations of degrees of equity and efficiency that are feasible? How much equity has to be sacrificed to obtain a given level of efficiency or vice versa? These kind of questions relate to the productive capacities of different kinds of social and economic organization, rather than to the values of the person making an assessment of them.

The 'productive capacity' of a society in terms of its ability to attain a given set of objectives is perhaps a slightly novel idea and deserves some amplification. First, it should not be confused with a more conventional interpretation of an economy's capacity in terms of the physical resources available to produce material commodities. Although undoubtedly constraints on physical resources will affect a society's ability to achieve its objectives, they will not be the only determinants of that ability. Other important determining factors are likely to include the society's economic system (whether it is predominantly capitalist, collectivist, mixed or whatever) and the psychological make-up of its inhabitants (whether they are individualistic or cooperative, materialist or ascetic, and so on). For instance, the combinations of equity and, say, economic growth attainable in a competitive market economy full of individualistic materialists might be rather different from those attainable in a cooperative economy run by and for ascetic altruists, even if both had the same initial resources.

The distinction between the value and the production trade-off can be illustrated in a simple diagram, such as that in Figure 3.1. Suppose there are two objectives, I and II, movement towards each of which can be measured by an index, X_I and X_{II}. In the figure, X_I is measured along the vertical axis and X_{II} along the horizontal axis. The convex lines, w_1, w_2 and w_3, are the indifference or 'welfare' contours for the policy-maker(s) or whoever is making the evaluation. Each contour connects points corresponding to all the combinations of I and II between which the policy-makers are indifferent; or, in other words, all the combinations that, in the relevant individuals' perceptions, yield the same level of 'social welfare'. Each contour thus corresponds to a particular level of social welfare, the level increasing with movement outwards from the origin. The slope of each contour represents the trade-off in terms of values between the two objectives: that is, how far society

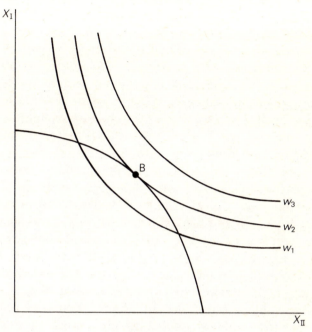

Figure 3.1

could move away from one objective in order to obtain a given movement in the direction of the other, without causing a fall in social welfare. The convexity of this slope represents the not unreasonable assumption that the closer society is to the attainment of one objective, the more it will be prepared to sacrifice in order to obtain a given movement in the direction of the other.

The concave line in Figure 3.1 refers to the society's productive capacity in terms of its objectives. It represents what might be termed the 'objective possibility frontier'.[1] All points on or within the frontier are feasible: that is, they represent combinations of values of the two indices that in principle could be attained by the society, given its constraints. Each point on the frontier shows, for a given value of one index, the maximum value of the other that the society can 'produce', given its resources, economic system, individuals' psychologies, etc. The slope of this line therefore represents the production trade-off: the amount of one index that would have to be sacrificed in order to obtain a given amount of the other. It is concave because it incorporates the assumption that this amount will decrease the higher the value of the index to be sacrificed: a reasonable assumption in most cases, but one that will not necessarily be true in all circumstances.

Point B (at which the objective possibility frontier is tangent to the welfare contour w_2) represents the 'best' combination of the two objectives for the society concerned. For, among all feasible combinations, this is the one that yields the highest possible level of welfare. At B the slope of the objective possibility frontier is equal to the slope of the relevant welfare contour (w_2); so at this point (but at this point only) the trade-offs are numerically equal.

It should be noted that this formulation is sufficiently general to be able to capture not only conceptualizations in terms of broad objectives, such as equity or liberty, but also the individualistic forms commonly found in the welfare economics literature. Suppose the 'objectives' of society are the raising of individual utilities. In that case the relationship between values and social welfare can be expressed in the standard formulation of a social welfare function postulating social welfare as a general function of individual utilities. In terms of Figure 3.1, X_j (j = I, II) represents the jth individual's utility, the contours are standard welfare contours and the objective possibility frontier is the utility possibility frontier. A utilitarian social welfare function can, of course, be represented as a special case of a Bergson–Samuelson function (and hence as a special case of Figure 3.1) with straight, negatively sloped welfare contours. Rawls's (1972) maximin or difference principle can also be represented in a similar fashion, with each individual's utilities (or more strictly, each individual's amount of primary goods) as the *X*s and with right-angled welfare contours.

So there are two forms of trade-off that have to be distinguished: the value trade-off and the production trade-off. They are distinct not only in conception, but also in the methods that it is necessary to use to establish their existence and magnitude. The magnitude of the value trade-off can only be established by reference to personal or social values; that of the production trade-off, in principle at least, by reference to empirical observation. At point B in Figure 3.1, the two will be equal; but equality does not imply identity.

Efficiency: an interpretation

The reader will have noted that the exposition of the diagram in Figure 3.1 did not refer to efficiency as an example of the objectives concerned. This was not because of a formalistic desire to remain within the abstract confines of algebraic notation. Rather, it was because the diagram suggests a definition of efficiency that seems a sensible interpretation of the meaning of the term, but one that would not be compatible with its being measured on the horizontal or vertical axes – or, more generally, with its being an objective that can be traded off against another, such as equity.

The definition is this. *An allocation of resources is efficient if it is impossible to move towards the attainment of one social objective without moving away from the attainment of another objective.* In terms of the diagram this implies that all points on the objective possibility frontier are efficient; whereas all points inside the frontier are inefficient.[2]

The better to understand the definition, consider a point such as R on Figure 3.2. This represents a combination of the indices that is inside the objective possibility frontier; it is an inefficient combination, because it is possible to increase the value of one index (thus moving towards one objective)

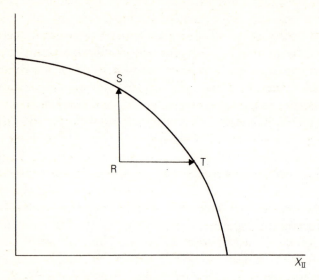

Figure 3.2

without reducing the value of the other (thus moving away from the second objective). Thus it is possible to reallocate resources so as to move society to point S, for example, increasing the value of X_I while keeping X_{II} constant; or to move to point T, increasing the value of X_{II} while keeping X_I constant. A movement to points on the frontier between S and T would increase both X_I and X_{II}. S, T and the points between them, on the other hand, represent efficient combinations of the two indices; for it is impossible to move from any of those points to any other feasible combination without reducing the value of at least one of the indices.

Economists will recognize that this interpretation of efficiency is a generalization of Pareto-optimality. In the Pareto case, the indices are interpreted in terms of individual utilities, and the objective possibility frontier becomes the utility possibility frontier. I shall return to the relationship between Pareto-optimality and equity below.

If the general interpretation of efficiency is accepted, what is the implication for the equity–efficiency trade-off? Simply that the notion of a trade-off, in either a value or production sense, is meaningless. For adopting this interpretation of efficiency implies that *efficiency can be defined only in relation to the ability of forms of social and economic organization to attain their primary objectives* and that therefore efficiency cannot itself be one of those primary objectives. In this sense, if equity is one of the objectives, it is meaningless to talk of a trade-off either in value or production between equity and efficiency. Efficiency is not an objective in the sense that equity is an objective; rather, it is a secondary objective that only acquires meaning with reference to primary objectives such as equity.[3]

Other interpretations of the equity–efficiency trade-off

What then do people generally mean when they are talking about the trade-off between equity and efficiency? For the reasons explained, they cannot be referring to a trade-off between equity and efficiency in the general sense of efficiency provided above; yet they clearly have some phenomenon in mind. The explanation has to be that they are using the term efficiency in some different way. One common interpretation is to identify efficiency with growth in aggregate economic production; another is to identify it with Pareto-optimality. Unfortunately, both create problems for the notion of the equity–efficiency trade-off.

Efficiency as economic growth

The identification of efficiency with economic growth is

widespread in both popular and academic discourse on the economy. Moreover, it is commonly asserted that the attainment of efficiency in the sense of economic growth is incompatible with the attainment of equity, and hence there is a trade-off between the two. Examples of this are legion: an influential one is Okun's eponymous *Equality and Efficiency: The Big Trade-off* (1975).[4]

A similar interpretation underlies many of the debates concerning the trade-off between efficiency and equity in the context of social security. A system of unemployment benefit that provides the unemployed with a basic income, may discourage people from seeking employment and hence from increasing their work effort; and if hours of work are reduced, so will economic growth be decreased. A system of state pensions may reduce the incentive of individuals to save to provide for their old age; unless this is offset by an increased propensity of the state to save, then this will result in smaller aggregate savings, smaller investment and hence a lower rate of economic growth.

This identification of efficiency with economic growth has an obvious appeal; and undoubtedly any 'production' trade-off between equity and economic growth that may exist would have serious policy implications. However, a single-minded concentration on growth does have its curious aspects. Increasing economic production does not seem a sensible objective on its own. Presumably, the only point of doing so is if the increase can be put to use: that is, if it can provide want-satisfaction (that is, generate utility) for one or more individuals. The relevant objective then becomes one of increasing individuals' utilities, presumably aggregated in some way.

Again it is of obvious importance to establish, as far as possible, the existence of any trade-off between equity and aggregate want-satisfaction. But there are complications. The exact method of aggregation has to be established. Is it to be a form of utilitarianism, with individual utilities being simply added together, or are they to be weighted in some way? Can utilities be 'added' in any reasonable fashion? These are standard problems, but their very familiarity does not mean they can be ignored.

Moreover, there are other, less well-known difficulties. For example, if the reason for identifying efficiency with economic production and thereby elevating it to the status of a primary objective is because increases in production lead to increases in individuals' utilities, then the utility *costs* of increased production should also be taken into account. Yet these are frequently neglected. The argument concerning the impact of social security on work effort, for example, often seems to ignore the possibility that work itself can have costs – that it may create disutility. This may have perverse consequences; an example is given in Appendix 3.1 where a particular social security change leads to an increase in money income, but also a fall in utility.

It is possible that much of the expressed concern about work incentives stems not so much from worries about aggregate production but from a perception by politicians and other policy-makers of a general reluctance among taxpayers to subsidize laziness – to give money apparently for nothing. In other words, a social security system that apparently encourages people not to work is thought to reduce the utility of those paying for it by more than if the payments did not apparently discourage work effort. In that case the supposed trade-off between equity and efficiency becomes a trade-off between increasing the utility of recipients and reducing the utilities of tax-payers; a trade-off that has meaning but one that seems a little way from the rather grander notions of equity versus efficiency.

In short, the identification of efficiency with economic growth, and hence its elevation to the status of a primary objective, indeed raises important issues concerning possible trade-offs with equity. But economic growth itself is far from unproblematic as an objective. Moreover, its identification with efficiency robs efficiency of the more general interpretation discussed in the previous section, an interpretation that concerns the ability of society to achieve any or all of its objectives. In many ways, it would seem preferable to divorce the idea of efficiency from that of economic growth and to discuss the issue of any trade-offs between growth and equity explicitly, rather than obscuring the issue by reference to efficiency.

Efficiency as Pareto-optimality

Another common interpretation of efficiency, at least among economists, is that of Pareto. Under this definition, an allocation of resources is efficient if it is impossible to make one individual better off without making another worse off. An allocation of resources with this property is described as Pareto-optimal or as Pareto-efficient. On this interpretation, an equity–efficiency trade-off will exist if there is no feasible allocation that is simultaneously equitable (according to a chosen definition of equity) and Pareto-optimal.

However, although commonly described in the relevant literature as a definition of efficiency, Pareto-optimality is more correctly interpreted as a form of value or social welfare function – one that, in certain forms, actually incorporates a notion of equity. This perhaps can be best illustrated by reference to the literature concerning 'potential' Pareto-optimality or the Hicks–Kaldor compensation principle. There it is asserted that there is an increase in welfare from a particular economic change if the gainers from the change can compensate the losers and still remain gainers. In the words of Hicks himself: 'if A is made so much better off by the change that he could compensate B for his loss, and still have something left over, then the reorganisation is an unequivocal improvement', a test that he goes on to describe as 'perfectly objective' (Hicks 1940–1, p. 108).

What this implies is that a potential Pareto-improvement

always constitutes an increase in welfare. One of the assumptions underlying this is a 'welfarist' one: that social welfare depends only on individuals' utilities. In terms of Figures 3.1 and 3.2, this implies that X_I and X_{II} refer to two individuals' utilities, and that therefore the objective possibility frontier is a utility possibility frontier.

Yet, more seriously, this identification of Pareto-improvements with increase in welfare implies that all points along the utility possibility frontier are equally 'good' in terms of welfare. But this can only be true if the *welfare contours have the same shape as the utility possibility frontier* – more specifically, if one of the welfare contours incorporating the values implicit in the social welfare function lies along the utility possibility frontier. In that case, the slope of the welfare contour must at all points be the same as the slope of the utility possibility frontier. And that implies a particular, and to many a rather unattractive, concept of equity: one in which a greater value is placed on increases in the utility of the better-off than on similar increases for the worse-off.

The formal proof of this last point is rather technical; it can be found in Appendix 3.1. But an intuitive understanding may be gleaned from the following example. Suppose there is a change of some kind that benefits a rich person by an amount estimated as £10, but also imposes a cost on a poor person of £9. Clearly, the rich person could fully compensate the poor person and remain a gainer. So, according to the compensation principle, whether or not the compensation actually takes place, there has been an increase in social welfare. But now consider the utility changes involved. On the not unreasonable assumption of diminishing marginal utility of income, if there is no compensation it is likely that the reduction in utility for the poor person due to the change is greater than the increase in utility for the rich person. Therefore, the only way that there could be a net increase in social welfare (in the absence of any actual compensation) is if the (smaller) change in utility for the rich person is 'weighted' in such a way that it increases welfare more than the (greater) utility change for the poor person reduces welfare. And this could only occur if the social welfare function weights rich people more (values them more) than poor people.

All this is an illustration of the general point that Pareto-optimality is perhaps better viewed as a specialized form of social welfare or value function, rather than as an 'objective' or universal definition of efficiency. In that case, investigations of the trade-offs between various interpretations of equity and Pareto-optimality are not really concerned with the trade-off between equity and efficiency at all. Instead they are investigating what is, at least in part, actually a trade-off between two different kinds of equity: that whose properties are being explored and that embodied in the Pareto social welfare function.

Conclusion

This chapter has made three main points. First, there are two types of trade-off to which the concept of an equity-efficiency trade-off could refer: a value and a production trade-off. In practice, it is often the latter that is of concern; but the two must be kept distinct.

Secondly, at least according to one general definition of efficiency – one that refers to society's ability to attain its primary objectives – the notion of a trade-off between equity and efficiency literally does not make sense; for trade-offs can only occur between these primary objectives, of which efficiency is not one.

Thirdly, even if efficiency is interpreted in such a way as to make it a primary objective, such as in terms of economic growth or of Pareto-optimality, there are serious problems in teasing out precisely what is being traded-off against what (in either value or production terms). Pareto-optimality, in particular, is more accurately viewed as a specialized form of social welfare function that itself incorporates a concept of equity; one that, under reasonable assumptions, can be shown to favour the better off. Hence any trade-off between Pareto-optimality and a given conception of equity is not one between efficiency and equity, but is, at least in part, a trade-off between two different kinds of equity.

A final point. It is conventional in economics to treat efficiency, in contrast to equity, as a concept that is relatively unproblematic. If this chapter has done nothing else, it has, I hope, demonstrated that this relative complacency is misplaced. The interpretation of efficiency is as much a complex and value-laden business as the interpretation of equity; a fact that complicates even more the interpretation of the trade-off between them.

Appendix 3.1

1 Incentives and social security: an illustration

In Figure 3.3, an individual's money income, y, is plotted along the vertical axis and her leisure, l, measured in hours, along the horizontal axis. It is assumed the individual can freely divide her hours between leisure and work. A social security system of the social dividend/negative income tax type is in operation, giving the individual a basic income whether or not she is in work, and taxing all earned income. The individual's only sources of income are earnings and social security.

Initially, the individual's after-tax-and-transfer budget constraint is given by ABC, where BC is the amount of the basic income. The individual is in equilibrium at point E on indifference curve U. A change in the system is then introduced that reduces the basic income to DC and reduces the

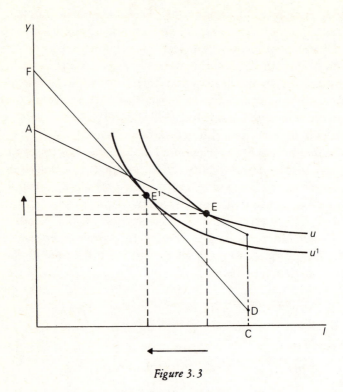

Figure 3.3

marginal tax rate, thus swivelling up the angled section of the budget line. The new budget line is now FDC; the new equilibrium, E^1 on indifference curve, U^1, with higher money income, less leisure (hence more work) – and lower utility. Hence, for this individual, the social security change has increased work effort, and the income derived from that work, but has reduced her overall level of satisfaction.

2 The social welfare function implicit in Pareto-optimality

Suppose there are two individuals, with utility functions u^1 and u^2 defined over money incomes, y^1 and y^2. Suppose there is only a fixed amount of total income, $y = y^1 + y^2$;

then the utility possibility frontier is:

$$y = f(u^1, u^2)$$

Differentiating this totally gives:

$$dy = \partial f/\partial u^1 \cdot du^1 + \partial f/\partial u^2 \cdot du^2$$

Along the frontier, $dy = 0$. Therefore the slope of the frontier ($- du^1/du^2$) is:

$$\frac{\partial f/\partial u^2}{\partial f/\partial u^1}$$

From the inverse function rule:

$$\partial u^1/\partial y^1 = \frac{1}{\partial f/\partial u^1} \text{ and } \partial u^2/\partial y^2 = \frac{1}{\partial f/\partial u^2}$$

Therefore:

$$- \frac{du^1}{du^2} = \frac{\partial u^1/\partial y^1}{\partial u^2/\partial y^2}$$

Thus the slope of the utility possibility frontier ($- du^1/du^2$) equals the ratio of the marginal utilities of income for the two individuals.

The Paretian social welfare function is a form of the general Bergson–Samuelson function, $W = W(u^1, u^2)$. Differentiating this totally gives:

$$dW = \partial W/\partial u^1 \cdot du^1 + \partial W/\partial u^2 \cdot du^2$$

Along each welfare contour, $dW = 0$. Therefore the slope of the contour ($- du^1/du^2$) is given by

$$\frac{\partial W/\partial u^2}{\partial W/\partial u^1}$$

If the utility possibility frontier lies along a welfare contour, as is required if all Pareto improvements are to constitute improvements in welfare, the slopes must be the same. Hence:

$$\frac{\partial W/\partial u^2}{\partial W/\partial u^1} = \frac{\partial u^1/\partial y^1}{\partial u^2/\partial y^2}$$

Thus the welfare weight attached in the social welfare function to a change in a given individual's utility varies inversely with that individual's marginal utility of income. If there is diminishing marginal utility of income, then this implies that the higher an individual's income, the higher the welfare weight. In other words, the social welfare function implicit in Pareto-optimality incorporates a conception of equity that favours the better-off (see also Varian 1984, for an alternative proof).

A more developed version of this argument, applying it to the measurement of changes in economic welfare, can be found in Le Grand (1984b) and Scafuri (1986).

Notes: Chapter 3

1   This terminology is doubly appropriate, in that the frontier is 'objective' both in the sense that it is concerned with society's objectives and in the sense that it is not based on subjective assessments of value.
2   This definition presumes that there is more than one social objective to be considered. If there is only one (as is the case, for instance, with utilitarianism) then the definition of an efficient allocation of resources becomes simply that which moves as close as possible to the attainment of the objective.
3   The argument that efficiency can only be defined in terms of wider objectives has an apparent similarity to that made in Goodin and Wilenski (1984). However, their point is rather different. They argue that efficiency as narrowly conceived by administrators (presumably, something like least resource cost) cannot be justified except by reference to what they term a meta-principle, such as want-satisfaction or respecting persons, and that, at times, pursuit of the meta-principle may require the overriding of the administrator's narrow conception of

efficiency. For the latter is simply one among many ways of satisfying the meta-principle: others include equity, democracy, due process, etc. But this is saying that equity and (one particular interpretation of) efficiency *are* objectives of similar status, which may have to be traded off against one another; quite different from the argument here, which provides an interpretation of efficiency in terms of the ability to attain *any* objective or set of objectives.

4 There are also variants on this identification of efficiency with growth. One example is Browning and Johnson (1984), where efficiency is apparently equated with growth in the disposable income of the highest three quintiles of the income distribution.

4   Methods of approach

The intention of the next two chapters is to evaluate different conceptions of equity. It is therefore important to specify the methods by which this evaluation is to be undertaken; and that is the task of this chapter.

Conceptual investigations of the kind proposed can take several forms. At one extreme, they could be entirely descriptive: an empirical enquiry into how a concept is actually used in everyday discourse. The aim here would be to uncover the 'true' meaning of the term concerned by reference to common usage; the methods would be those of empirical investigation: the illustrative example, the case study, the survey. At the other extreme would be a study that aimed at a prescriptive or stipulative definition: a definition that prescribes, rather than describes, the meaning of a concept. The intention here is to take a concept that 'still remains to be *moulded* and ... to mould the unmoulded meanings, to make fixed and sharp that which ordinary usage leaves loose and undetermined' (von Wright 1963, p. 5; emphasis in original). The methods used in this kind of investigation are more difficult to specify: von Wright summarizes them as simply 'philosophical reflexion' (ibid).

Now the task of defining equity cannot be a wholly empirical one. This is partly for pragmatic reasons; as we shall see, some of the conventional empirical approaches are difficult to apply in this context, if not wholly useless. But, perhaps more important, it is because, inevitably with a concept as widely employed as that of equity, there is a laxity in usage, there are conflicting interpretations, there are areas of vagueness that will remain even if a measure of consistency can be identified. Hence, any formulation or definition of equity will inevitably to some extent be prescriptive.

However, it is one of the contentions of this book that, although the concept of equity is used in many different contexts and apparently takes a wide variety of meanings in these contexts, it does not fall into the category of concepts that 'remain to be moulded' – at least not completely. Rather, there is a core of consistency in the way that the term is used in everyday discourse: a core that is not always easy to perceive, but that exists nonetheless. The task in front of us is therefore closer to the first extreme than the second – although, for the reasons given, it is not *at* that extreme.

Given that we are undertaking a kind of empirical exercise – attempting to discover a core of consistency in the way the term equity is actually used – how should we proceed? There seem to be three principal methods of approach. The first is the test of intuition through what has been termed the 'case-implication' critique; the second, through an 'impartiality' mechanism such as the social contract device used by Rawls (1972); the third, by more conventional empirical investigations where people are actually questioned concerning their beliefs or values, or those beliefs and values are inferred through systematic observation of their actions. This chapter looks at each of these in turn. Finally, there is a brief discussion of other criteria that have been suggested for evaluating conceptions of equity.

The test of intuition

The essence of this approach can be simply stated. The aim is to find a definition of equity that will command general agreement. An essential requirement of such a definition is that it should not lead 'most people', for whom the reader has to act as a representative, to judge as equitable situations which their moral intuitions would regard as inequitable, or vice versa. Any definition which did result in such a conflict would, ipso facto, not command a consensus: for, to be acceptable, a proposed definition has to conform to the moral implications of the term.

This is of particular importance if an interpretation of equity is to be found that will be useful for policy purposes. For to arrive at a definition by any other route risks introducing policies that are supposedly equitable but actually have outcomes that are judged by the relevant individuals as inequitable, or correcting apparently inequitable policies in a direction that makes them less, rather than more, equitable.

To argue for the importance of intuition is in apparent conflict with some philosophers' rejection of 'intuitionism' as a means of establishing moral principles; see, for instance, Hare (1981). But the disagreement is more apparent than real. In the work cited, Hare objects to the use of intuition as a means of establishing the essential 'right-ness' of moral propositions; he also points out that it offers little help in cases where moral propositions conflict. However, he accepts (p. 13) that intuition has a role in determining what people actually mean when they use moral terminology. Since the aim is to find a definition of equity that will command a measure of consensus, it is precisely this role that intuition is playing here; for, to command a consensus, it is necessary to establish a definition that accords with the way in which the term is generally used. In Hare's terminology the appeal is to linguistic intuitions rather than moral ones.

How do we set about the process of appealing to intuition? The most commonly employed technique is what Sen (1982) has termed the case-implication critique. This is where the implications of applying a conceptual principle to a particular case or instance are drawn out, and the results compared with intuition to see whether they harmonize. If they do harmonize – that is, if there is no conflict between the judgements concerning the case that flow from the application of the principle and those that flow from intuition – then the principle is supported; if not, its usefulness is weakened, if not destroyed.[1]

Now it is likely that direct appeals to intuition are a form of reasoning with which many social scientists will feel unhappy. The case-implication critique *feels* unsystematic. It is not empirical in the sense in which the term is usually used in the social sciences in that it does not refer to observable data. It is not even axiomatic or deductive. It might be thought preferable to concentrate on apparently more scientific methodologies, such as the impartiality mechanism of the social contract or the actual empirical observation of people's beliefs. But do either of these in fact offer a superior alternative?

The social contract

On this approach, principles are evaluated by reference to the choices that individuals might make if they were in a 'state of nature', drawing up a social contract: a set of binding principles or rules for the society that they are all to inhabit. It is a version of what Sen (1982) has called the 'prior principle' approach, where a conception is justified by reference to a prior principle: in this case, decisions taken under the social contract.

The principal recent exponent of the social contract is Rawls (1972). Other examples of the prior principle approach include the notion of dialogue developed by Ackerman (1980), and the similar conception of Habermas (1976) of undistorted rational discourse, where principles are first established concerning the acceptability of types of arguments in moral discourse, and then the arguments for and against particular value conceptions and principles are evaluated with reference to those principles. Since all of these rely on the notion of the prior principle and therefore have a fundamental similarity, I shall concentrate on the social contract to illustrate the relevant points.

Under the social contract, a particular principle is justified if it would be chosen by a group of individuals drawing up a social contract (a set of principles by which a society is organized) in the 'initial position'. This is a situation where

> no-one knows his place in society, his class position or social status, nor does anyone know his fortune in the distribution of natural assets and abilities, his intelligence, strength and the like. [Nor do they know] ... their conceptions of the good or their special psychological propensities. The principles of justice are chosen behind a veil of ignorance. (Rawls 1972, p. 12)

A possible advantage of this approach is that it appears to be based on logic rather than on intuition. At least in the first instance, principles are not evaluated with respect to outcomes; they are deduced, via a process of logical reasoning through a specific procedure. There is scope for assessing the logic of the reasoning; or, by applying the reasoning to different underlying pre-conditions, to discover different conceptions or principles.

However, this advantage is more apparent than real. The use of intuition has not been avoided. As Rawls himself says:

> There is, however, another side to justifying a particular (set of principles). That is to see if the principles ... chosen match our considered convictions of justice or extend them in an acceptable way. We can note whether applying these principles would lead us to make the same judgements about the basic structure of society which we now make

intuitively, and in which we have the greatest confidence. (Rawls 1972, p. 19).

If the principles derived from the initial position

> match our considered convictions of justice, then so far well and good. But presumably there will be discrepancies. In this case we have a choice. We can either modify the account of the initial situation or we can revise our existing judgements, for even the judgements we take provisionally as fixed points are liable to revision. By going back and forth, sometimes altering the conditions of the contractual circumstances, at others withdrawing our judgements and conforming them to principle, I assume that eventually we shall find a description of the initial situation that both expresses reasonable conditions and yields principles which match our considered judgements duly pruned and adjusted. This state of affairs I refer to as reflective equilibrium. (Rawls 1972, p. 20)

Thus, as with the case implication critique, intuition has a crucial role to play. It is used to evaluate the outcomes of the social contract procedure, and, if necessary, altering the circumstances under which the contract has been drawn up so as to achieve the desired (i.e. intuition compatible) result. This process of obtaining 'reflective equilibrium' has been described by Brian Barry as one where:

> we fiddle about with the conditions of the original position until they produce the deductions that we want to get out. At a minimum, that is to say, we have to keep adjusting them so that the principles deduced from them do not conflict with our unshakable 'common-sense' convictions of right and wrong. (Barry 1973, p. 12)

Moreover, this is not the only role that intuition plays in

the procedure. It also arises in assessing what conditions are likely to obtain in the 'initial position' where the social contract is drawn up. As Rawls himself says, 'there are ... many possible interpretations of the initial situation' and it is necessary to choose 'the one interpretation ... which best expresses the conditions that are *widely thought reasonable* to impose on the choices of principles' (Rawls 1972, p. 121; emphasis added). But, as many writers (both before and after Rawls) have shown, there are several possible conditions whose application to the initial position could be widely thought 'reasonable'; and, if one's intuitions about reasonableness differ from Rawls's, quite different principles emerge. Rawls's maximin or difference principle, for instance, under which resources should be allocated so as to maximize the position of the least well-off (discussed in more detail in Chapter 5), derives from his belief that individuals in the initial position would evaluate principles of justice as though they were *certain* that their eventual position in society would be as the least well-off: an intuitive judgement he later supported on the grounds that the individuals concerned would be making decisions about their whole life position and thus could not afford to take any risk (Rawls 1974). But if, as seems quite possible, intuition suggests that individuals in the initial position would make their evaluation based on an assumption that each outcome is equi-probable, then, even if they are risk averse, the principles derived would not necessarily be maximin in form; rather, they could take on a variety of possibilities including Rawls's principal target for criticism, utilitarianism (Harsanyi 1955; Arrow 1973; Sugden and Weale 1979; Weale 1983, ch. 5).

Thus, under the social contract, intuition, so far from being avoided, has a double role to play. It has to be used to assess the conditions of the initial position, *and* to evaluate the outcomes of the deliberations of the individuals in that position.[2] The same is true of the other 'prior principle' approaches of Ackerman and Habermas. For, at the end of the day, the legitimacy of the basic principles that guide their versions of rational dialogue can only be established according to their intuitive acceptability; similarly, the outcomes of the dialogues themselves have to be intuitively acceptable. There seems to be no advantage here over the case-implication technique; indeed, it is likely that something like the latter would have to be used as part of the outcome evaluation process. The social contract, and the other versions of the prior principle approach, do not therefore seem to be superior to the more direct test of intuition involved in the case-implication technique.

Empirical observation

There are several empirical approaches to the discovery of people's beliefs and values. One, used principally by social psychologists, is experimental, whereby selected subjects are asked to make judgements concerning the justice of different situations in laboratory 'experiments'. A second, used by empirical sociologists, is the household survey, where people are asked questions concerning their beliefs and values. A third, adopted primarily by economists, is to infer beliefs concerning values from observation of collective behaviour in actual situations; in particular, they have concentrated on government taxation and expenditure decisions as instances of collective expressions of values.

The principal intention of the work of social psychologists has been to discover whether people make equity judgements differently in different situations and, if so, the reasons for the differences. The methodology employed is experimental, involving paid subjects performing tasks in laboratories. Examples include Webster and Smith (1978), Törnblom and Foa (1983) and Stolte (1987); Deutsch (1985) and Soltan (1982) give useful reviews. To understand its strengths and weaknesses, it is useful to give an example of

the approach in action. It should be remembered that, as
mentioned in an earlier chapter, social psychologists use the
term justice where we use the term equity; they confine
equity to one specific interpretation, 'to each according to his
merit (contribution)' (Deutsch 1985, p. 2).

What seems to be a reasonably typical experiment is
described in Deutsch (1985, pp. 164–5). In this case, the
aim of the research was to discover whether groups that were
production oriented would choose different distribution
principles from solidarity-oriented groups. Eighty male US
undergraduates participated in two-person groups. Half the
groups were told that the intention of the research was to
determine how productive people were under various conditions; the groups were encouraged to work as efficiently as
possible. The other half was told that the research was concerned with the process of friendship formation; they were
encouraged to get to know each other as well as possible
while they worked. Each pair were then set four hidden word
puzzles to solve. At the end of the tasks, the subjects filled
out a questionnaire, whose primary purpose – the real
purpose of the research – was to establish how the subject
thought the groups' earnings should be divided. The results
showed a small, but statistically significant, difference
between the two halves, with the solidarity groups favouring
equality as a distributive principle and the production oriented groups favouring a distribution based on contribution.[3]

In fact, this kind of outcome seems to be one of the
principal conclusions of this work. In reviewing this and
other similar experiments, Deutsch summarizes the findings
as follows:

> The preference for sociocentric principles of distributive
> justice (such as egalitarianism and generosity) is associated
> with positive social-emotional, solidarity-oriented social
> relations, whereas the preference for individual-centred
> principles (such as proportionality or equity) is associated

with impersonal task-directed, economic social relations. (Deutsch 1985, p. 202; typographical error corrected)

These findings related primarily to the distribution of one commodity (money) in one social context (work) and to the views of one particular group (American college students). Other work of this kind suggests that people's views of the appropriate principle of justice to be applied in different situations may vary according to the commodity or attribute to be distributed, and the context of the distribution. Moreover, there is little consistency in the results across different kinds of people, with the outcomes varying according to nationality, occupation and the degree of success achieved. For example, one study found that successful American business people tended to prefer all attributes (broadly defined to include love and status, as well as money) to be distributed according to contribution; unsuccessful business people agreed with their more successful counterparts that money should be allocated according to contribution, but not love or status; Swedish students preferred equality in everything, with allocations according to contribution always being viewed negatively (Törnblom and Foa 1983).

Although undoubtedly this kind of research is important and suggestive, it also has obvious limitations. For instance, it is not always possible to tell from the reports of the results whether the subjects, in making their judgements concerning the desirability of different hypothetical distributional principles, were always able to distinguish between the requirements of equity or justice and those of other concerns (such as incentives). Törnblom, Jonsson and Knowles (1982) conducted an experiment where subjects were asked twice how much four people whose performance on a creativity test differed should be paid; once their 'overall' assessment, and once if the only criterion was one of justice. Responses to the first task allocated pay according to performance; responses to the second allocated it equally. Commenting on the results, Törnblom and Foa observe (1983, p. 162): 'If unravelling the various meanings subjects may attach to the notion of justice is problematic to researchers in the area, the separation and interpretation of the motives' underlying responses... (where the goal of justice is not specified and required) and their relations to justice evaluations is, indeed, a formidable task to tackle.' (Even the researchers themselves may occasionally face this problem, as indicated by the quotation above from Deutsch, where 'generosity' is included as a principle of justice, whereas as noted in Chapter 2 it is actually something rather different.)

Another objection concerns representativeness. The subjects are commonly US college students: hardly representative samples of the population of the United States, let alone of other countries. The second approach, that of the empirical sociologist using the social survey, partly overcomes this difficulty, although again this has been confined largely to North America.[4] The work either involves the secondary analysis of data collected for other purposes, or directly undertakes household interviews, of varying degrees of intensity, to ascertain respondents' views about social justice. Examples include Robinson and Bell (1978), Alves and Rossi (1978), Schlozman and Verba (1979), Hochschild (1981), McClosky and Zaller (1984), Kluegel and Smith (1986), Marshall et al. (1988) and Bellah et al. (1988).[5]

Again it is useful briefly to describe one of these to illustrate the strengths and weaknesses of the approach. The study by Alves and Rossi (1978) may be taken as reasonably representative. They undertook a random sample of 522 American adults. The respondents were asked standard socio-economic information about themselves and the households in which they lived; but their principal task was to judge the fairness of fifty or so 'vignettes'. The vignettes were computer-generated descriptions of fictitious households, with characteristics picked out at random. The characteristics included, for each adult member of the household, educational attainment, occupation, race, gender and marital status, and, for the household as a whole, number of children and annual earnings (gross and net of tax). Each respondent was asked to judge the relative fairness of each vignette on a nine point scale of fairness. The fairness ratings were then regressed on the characteristics of the 'vignette' households to see whether there was any consistency in the association between fairness judgements and those characteristics. The sample was also divided into subgroups according to the income and social status of the respondents and the regressions were run separately from each subgroup.

The results showed that the characteristics of vignette households explained around half of the variation in respondents' fairness judgements: a high proportion for cross-section regression exercises of this kind. Most of the characteristics were statistically significant; the principal exceptions were, interestingly, gender and race, neither of which appeared to play a significant role in determining fairness judgements. There were statistically significant differences between the subgroups, but these were small.

The researchers described education and occupation as 'merit' indicators and marital status and number of children as indicators of 'need'. They interpreted their results as supporting the view that both merit and need have an important role to play in determining most people's judgements of the fairness of different situations – although they did find disagreement as to how these principles should be applied in different situations. Overall, the results were sufficiently strong to make them consider it legitimate to conclude that 'previous research traditions ... have presumed the existence of a consensual normative framework for making distributive-justice judgements: they may proceed assured that such a framework does exist' (Alves and Rossi 1978, pp. 562–3).

Despite the attempt to attain a greater degree of representativeness than the laboratory studies, this kind of work still encounters the problem that different studies yield different conclusions. The findings of the study by Bellah *et al.* (1988) of the values of the American middle class found that, as with Alves and Rossi, there was agreement on abstract principles such as freedom, equality and merit, but there was no common perception of how these principles were implemented in practice. On the other hand, McClosky and Zaller (1984) interpret the outcomes of the various studies that they examine as showing that 'the values of the American ethos frequently conflict with one another and lead to opposing policy prescriptions' (p. 286) – in direct contrast to the conclusion reached by Alves and Rossi. Other research has shown systematic variation in people's values concerning issues of justice by race, gender, income, class and educational attainment (Kluegel and Smith 1986; Robinson and Bell 1978).

Moreover, not only does there appear to be variation between different individuals' beliefs, but there seem to be inconsistencies within the individuals themselves. Marshall *et al.* (1988), for example, in a comprehensive study of British class attitudes, found apparent inconsistencies between peoples' beliefs concerning social justice in abstract and beliefs concerning their own position. More generally, the researchers 'pursued issues of logical, technical, normative and ideological congruence across a wide variety of attitudes and beliefs and after a lengthy investigation arrived firmly at the conclusion that people can quite unconcernedly hold contradictory beliefs' (Marshall 1990, p. 28).

These differences both between people and within individuals themselves may arise not because of actual inconsistencies, but because of the difficulty of elucidating sophisticated concepts by an interview procedure (or indeed a laboratory one). The unravelling of complex ideas such as those relating to principles of distributive justice perhaps requires longer periods of reflection and debate than a survey interview can provide. Further, as with the laboratory experiments, it is not always easy to ascertain the extent to which a commitment to a particular position reflects beliefs concerning justice or beliefs concerning other matters, such as the importance of incentives. As discussed in Chapter 3, apparent inconsistencies in distributive judgements can arise because people can quite consistently make different trade-offs between conflicting values in different situations.

A different kind of objection to both the laboratory and the survey approach concerns the hypothetical nature of the situations posed. Individuals may react differently to real-life situations where equity judgements are concerned and where the making of those judgements has (possibly serious) consequences for themselves or for others. To ascertain what people 'really' mean by equity, rather than observing their behaviour in a variety of situations where the final outcome is irrelevant to their (or anyone else's) lives, it might be preferable to observe what happens when they are required to take an equity judgement that has actual consequences.

However, the observation of 'real-life' situations brings with it its own problems. The most obvious of these concerns the difficulty of disentangling the motives of those involved; in particular, those relating to self-interest, as distinct from those concerned with broader moral principles. Thus, poor individuals may make an impassioned claim that they should receive a larger share of economic resources and will back this up with a series of moral arguments concerning equity; but it would be difficult to know whether those arguments really captured their interpretation of equity, or whether they were simply firing off any ammunition they could find in order to pursue their own self-interest. Impartiality is difficult to sustain when one's own interests are affected.

One way of attempting to overcome this problem is not to observe the behaviour of individuals themselves, but to observe that of a supposedly impartial guardian of individuals' interests, such as a democratically elected government. Virtually all decisions taken by governments have equity consequences; could not those decisions be analysed in some way in order to yield the value assumptions that lie behind them?

A further advantage of this process, if it were feasible, is that it might go some way towards meeting the objection of unrepresentativeness levelled against the hypothetical laboratory situations; whatever the defects of the democratic process, the actions of a democratic government are likely to be representative of the views and values of a wider range of people than those involved in most laboratory experiments.

Several analyses of this kind have been undertaken by economists. The procedure is to assume that the government, in formulating a given policy, acts according to a particular principle or maximizes a particular form of social welfare function; then to 'invert' the problem by calculating from the observed structure of the policy itself what the values of certain parameters would have to be if the policy were constructed on the assumed principle or social welfare function. Thus Preinreich (1943), Haveman (1965) and Mera (1969) have calculated the value of relative marginal utilities of income implicit in the US tax schedule on the assumption that the government set that schedule according to one or other of the 'sacrifice' principles of taxation, while Dickinson (1953) and Stern (1977) have produced estimates based on similar methodologies for the British income tax.[6] Christiansen and Jansen (1978) have estimated the extent of inequality aversion implicit in the Norwegian indirect tax system, and the social or 'welfare' weights applied to a marginal increase in income for each household, on the assumption that the system is the outcome of maximizing a specific social welfare function; Ahmad and Stern (1984) used a similar procedure to calculate welfare weights derived from the Indian indirect tax system. Weisbrod (1968) estimated welfare weights from observation of actual government expenditure decisions; Dasgupta, Marglin and Sen (1972) suggested that weights could be derived from a dialogue between 'ministers' and 'planners', where the planners provide ministers with a description of alternative projects and infer the latter's preferences from their choices. Le

Grand (1975b) estimated the relative marginal utilities of income implicit in the means-tests applied to two British government expenditure programmes. The procedure has been discussed by Musgrave (1959), Eckstein (1961) and, most recently, by Drèze and Stern (1985) who term it the 'inverse optimum' approach; the theoretical structure is laid out, and the procedure criticized, in Basu (1980).

The procedures involved are rather technical and examples of them have therefore been relegated to Appendix 4.1. But the studies concerned can be criticized on a number of grounds. First, most of them try to derive numbers for some highly specific parameters (such as relative marginal utilities of income), rather than attempting to elucidate wider principles of equity or distributive justice.[7] These parameters will only be useful for equity purposes under specific circumstances. The values of the relative marginal utilities of income would be useful, for example, for a utilitarian conception of equity, where a distribution of income would be considered equitable if it was the outcome of maximizing a utilitarian social welfare function. In that case, the weights that would be attached to individuals' incomes in calculating improvements in overall welfare would be the marginal utilities of income. However, they would not be useful for the application of any non-utilitarian conception of equity.

But a more fundamental problem is that of inconsistency. My own study (Le Grand 1975b), for instance, showed that the values of the relative marginal utilities implicit in two government programmes (one concerned with housing and one with education) were quite different; they were also different *within* the same programme, when that programme was investigated at two separate but close points in time. This does not inspire confidence in the techniques as a means of eliciting stable values incorporating equity (or indeed any other) judgements.

Nor is this very surprising. The key assumption, that government is a unitary agent with well-defined values and beliefs, is inherently implausible. Policy outcomes are the result of a complex interaction between individuals and groups with widely differing interests, powers and beliefs. As Basu has argued:

> It ... is trivially obvious that a government is a complex organisation, consisting of various departments, which often have widely divergent aims. Its leadership is not permanent. Even when there is no overt change in leadership, there are shifts in the balance of power which may alter a government's motivation ... Also, once the government is recognised as having a multiplicity of aims and various departments and wings, it becomes difficult to *identify* the government. In an idealised situation there is a clear set of policy-makers who take the ultimate decisions based on evaluation done by project formulators and evaluators... [but]... in reality it is difficult to say who makes the policies. The ministers may take the final decision but they are influenced by interest groups and lobbies. Once the nebulous structure of governments is recognised, doubts arise about the meaningfulness of talking about governmental preference and rationality, or the lack of it. (Basu 1980, pp. 57–8; emphasis in original)

Conclusion

From this discussion of the possible methodological approaches to obtaining and evaluating conceptions of equity, it is difficult to escape the conclusion that there is only one that is really suitable: the test of intuition. The reliance upon readers' intuitions is not avoided – indeed it is compounded – by the social contract approach, perhaps its chief philosophical competitor. And approaches that might be more favoured by social scientists, ones that involve direct empirical investigation, are too crude, too hypothetical, or, as with the revelation of government preferences approach, too unrealistic in their fundamental assumptions to be of use for our purposes.

Finally, it should be noted that several other, rather different, kinds of criteria have been suggested as a basis for evaluating different conceptions of equity. Rawls (1974) mentions two: that the conception should have relatively low information requirements and that it should be comprehended easily. Others that might appeal to economists are summarized by Pazner and Schmeidler (1978). Discussing a particular definition of equity, they argue that it is 'appealing from an equity viewpoint in that it treats economic agents symmetrically, is ordinal in nature and free of interpersonal comparisons of utility'. Another criterion, they add, is that 'in the light of the general acceptance of the Pareto criterion, it would be desirable to have a concept of equity that never conflicts with Pareto-efficiency' (p. 672).

The eccentricity of the requirement that a conception of equity should never conflict with Pareto-optimality is discussed in Chapter 5. The other criteria – symmetry, ordinality, avoiding interpersonal comparisons of utility, low information requirements and ease of comprehension – are of more relevance; but they do seem essentially secondary to intuition for accepting or rejecting conceptions of equity. However easily understood a conception may be, or however little it requires by way of information, it is going to be of little use if it conflicts with people's fundamental beliefs about what is equitable or fair. The ultimate test of any interpretation of equity has to be whether or not it conforms to those beliefs.

Appendix 4.1 The inverse optimum approach

As two illustrations of the inverse optimum approach, this

appendix briefly summarizes the methodologies of the tax studies and the (rather different) methodology of my own study.

Each of the tax studies assumes that a given income tax schedule is drawn up on the basis of one or more of the 'sacrifice' principles of taxation. These principles require that the tax paid by each taxpayer should have a similar impact in terms of the utility sacrificed. Thus Preinreich (1948) assumed the principle was equal proportional sacrifice (the tax causes the same proportional loss in utility for all tax-payers); Haveman (1965) used a version of equal marginal sacrifice (the rate of change of sacrifice with income should be the same); Mera (1969) produced two sets of estimates, one based on the assumption of equal proportional sacrifice and the other on equal absolute sacrifice (the absolute loss in utility caused by the tax should be the same). Dickinson (1953) used a version of equal proportional sacrifice; Stern (1977), equal marginal sacrifice.

The methodology can be illustrated by the use of the principle of equal absolute sacrifice. This requires that:

$$u^i(y^i) - u(y^i - T^i) = k \qquad (4.1)$$

where u^i is the ith individual's utility function, y^i, her income before tax, T^i is her tax payment, and k is constant for all individuals. Differentiating (4.1) with respect to income gives:

$$\partial u^i/\partial y^i - \partial u^i/\partial(y^i - T^i)(1 - \partial T^i/\partial y^i) = 0$$

where $\partial T^i/\partial y^i$ is the marginal tax rate. Rearranging:

$$1 - \partial T^i/\partial y^i = \frac{\partial u^i/\partial y^i}{\partial u^i/\partial(y^i - T^i)} \qquad (4.2)$$

The right-hand side of (4.2) is the ratio of the marginal utilities of income before and after tax. Since the left-hand side can be calculated for any level of pre-tax income from observation of the income tax schedule, this can be used to derive the value of that ratio implicit in the schedule.

The Le Grand (1975b) study concerned means-tested public programmes: programmes where the price charged for a public service varies with the income of the recipient. The aim of most such programmes is to ensure a certain level of take-up of the service. If it is assumed that (a) the utility derived by individuals from the use of the service concerned is independent of their consumption of other goods and services and (b) that individual utility functions are identical, then the marginal utility of the service at any level of use will be the same for all individuals. In that case the price charged in order to ensure that all individuals consume the desired amount of the service should vary so that the marginal utility of that price is the same for all: a condition that in turn requires the price to be inversely proportional to the marginal utility of income.

Thus, if $\partial u^i / \partial x^i$ is the marginal utility to the ith individual of the service, the amount of which is denoted x^i, then from the first order conditions of utility maximization:

$$\partial u^i / \partial x^i = \lambda^i . p^i \qquad (4.3)$$

where λ^i is the marginal utility of income to the individual and p^i is the price that she faces. If $\partial u^i / \partial x^i$ is constant for all individuals, then (4.3) implies that, for any two individuals i and j:

$$\frac{p^i}{p^j} = \frac{\lambda^j}{\lambda^i} \qquad (4.4)$$

(4.4) can then be applied to an observed price scale to calculate the relative marginal utilities of income implicit in that scale.

Notes: Chapter 4

1 The case-implication technique is not the only way of appealing to intuition. Another is the mental or thought experiment where readers are asked to imagine themselves in a situation where it is necessary to specify their values. One example of this is Okun's 'leaky bucket' experiment (Okun 1975, pp. 91–5; see also Atkinson 1983b, pp. 56–9). This involves a hypothetical programme that redistributes income from rich to poor, but in which there is a certain amount of leakage from the bucket carrying the money, so that for every pound taken from the rich less than a pound gets to the poor. Readers are asked to decide how much leakage they would be prepared to accept from the redistribution programme and still continue to support the programme.
   The value being specified in Okun's particular experiment is not actually a principle of equity but a specific parameter characterizing the magnitude of the trade-off between 'efficiency' (defined as in terms of aggregate output) and equality of incomes that readers are prepared to accept. However, there is no reason why thought experiments of a more general kind could not be followed to establish principles of equity; indeed, as we shall see shortly, the social contract is just such an experiment.

2 David Miller has pointed out to me (personal communication) that, although this is an accurate description of Rawls's position, a thoroughgoing contractarian might refuse to be bothered by conflicts between common intuitions and the results of the social contract thought experiment. Then the plausibility of the argument would be totally dependent on the intuitive acceptability of the way in which the contract situation was set up.

3 The researchers were a little puzzled that the differences were small; but they explained it by the cooperative context in which all the groups operated, even the production oriented ones (Deutsch 1985, p. 166).

4 As far as I am aware there have been relatively few attempts to ascertain people's beliefs concerning the meaning of equity by the use of this method outside the United States. However, a major research project comparing beliefs about distributive justice across a wide variety of countries is under way at the time of writing (Perceptions of Justice in East and West, coordinated by David Mason, Butler University, Indianapolis). Also, in Britain there have been several surveys of

attitudes towards related policy issues such as taxation, welfare spending and incomes policies, whose results could be used to shed some light on values concerning distribution. Examples are Golding and Middleton (1982), Taylor-Gooby (1985), and Jowell *et al.* (1989).

5 This literature is very usefully reviewed in Marshall (1990).

6 The marginal utility of income to an individual is the extra satisfaction that she derives from a small increase in her income.

7 In this respect they are similar to Okun's leaky bucket experiment; see note 1.

5 Economic conceptions of equity

Many interpretations of an equitable distribution have appeared in the works of the writers who have concerned themselves with the issue, and it would be impossible to do full justice to all of them here (or indeed to treat them all equitably). Instead, I concentrate on some of the principal ideas that have attracted recent attention in the economics literature and, through the use of the case implication approach discussed in the previous chapter, show why they do not capture, or at least do not capture fully, the essence of the concept of equity. I call them 'economic' conceptions not only because they are among the principal conceptions used by economists in discussing equity issues, but also because, not coincidentally, they are generally applied in the context of the distribution of economic resources, such as income or wealth.

Specifically, I shall discuss: equity defined in terms of equality of outcome, with particular reference to income and utility; equity as envy-freeness; the 'rank-reversal' interpretation of horizontal equity; and the conceptions of equity implicit in the larger philosophical schemes of the utilitarians and of John Rawls, both of which have received a great deal of attention from economists. I also consider briefly two other principles that have been suggested as guides to distributional policy but that are not based explicitly on notions of equity or justice: so-called Pareto-optimal redistribution and the libertarian principle of voluntarism.

Political philosophers confronted with this list might be rather surprised, both at what is included and what is omitted. Some of the ideas included have received little attention from philosophers; while several principles that have been the focus of intense philosophical debate are omitted, such as those based on conceptions of needs or deserts, equality of opportunity, equality of resources and so on. Social psychologists or empirical sociologists working in the area might be equally surprised at the omission of ideas such as need and desert, which their empirical investigations suggest play an important role in many people's perceptions of equity, as we saw in the previous chapter.

But the list is on the whole a reasonable reflection of the literature in economics. The fact that in this literature considerable attention is paid to some relatively unknown principles, while more obvious ones are neglected, is far from accidental. As this chapter will try to demonstrate, on the whole economists have not based the conceptions of equity that they use on moral intuitions; a lacuna which means that, almost inevitably, they have tended at times to use principles that may have little intuitive resonance, while ignoring ones that may be prominent among those intuitions.[1] In the next chapter, an equity principle is put forward that, it is argued, is more acceptable intuitively than those discussed in this chapter; and there the relationship of the principle to other intuitively based conceptions, including several of those not discussed in this chapter, will be discussed in some detail.

Equality of outcome

Chapter 2 drew attention to the fact there is no automatic link between equity and equality. Nonetheless, it is common to see the two identified with one another. In particular, equity is frequently interpreted as requiring equality of outcome in either of two kinds: *equality of income* and *equality of utility*.

To begin with equality of income. Suppose we observe three individuals, Amanda, Barbara and Catherine. Barbara and Catherine have the same income, but Amanda has an income greater than both. If that was *all* we knew about their respective situations we might be tempted to judge the income difference as inequitable; indeed, if equity is interpreted in terms of equality of income, we would be required to do so. But now suppose we learn that Amanda and Barbara have identical opportunities to obtain income: they are equally skilled, work in the same job and have no restrictions on the amount of time they can work. The reason why Barbara has a lower income than Amanda is simply because she has chosen to work less hard; to spend more time on leisure activities and less on income generation. Would we then consider the outcome in terms of their difference in incomes to be inequitable?

Suppose that we also acquired some information about Catherine. She is similar to Amanda and Barbara with regard to her skills and her freedom to work; and she works as hard as Amanda. But she has a lower income than Amanda because Amanda is white while Catherine, with identical skills and preferences, is black and working for a racially prejudiced employer. In that case, it is likely that we would judge the gap in income between Amanda and Catherine as less equitable than the *same* gap in income between Amanda and Barbara.

This example suggests that there can be no automatic identification of unequal *incomes* with inequity; nor equal incomes with equity. However, to overcome objections of this kind, it might be argued that the focus of concern should be on equality of *utilities* or satisfactions rather than on incomes. In the example considered, Barbara's level of utility may well be on a par with Amanda's, although they have derived it from different combinations of income and leisure. Therefore, the difference between their respective situations would not, on this interpretation, constitute inequity.

That an allocation of resources is equitable in which utilities are equal has considerable intuitive appeal, and has formed the basis of several important contributions to the economics literature: for example, the equity axioms of Sen (1973) and Hammond (1976, 1977). These axioms are rules for distributing income to increase the value of what Hammond (1977, p. 52) terms 'equity-regarding' social welfare functions: functions which show an increase in welfare when, *ceteris paribus*, the difference between any two individuals' utilities is decreased.[2]

But this interpretation also has its problems. Its information requirements are considerable; in particular, utilities have to be observable, measurable and interpersonally comparable. A more important difficulty is one discussed extensively in some recent contributions to the philosophical literature (Dworkin 1981a; Cohen 1989; Barry 1990): people with preferences that are very expensive to satisfy. For example, a cultivated connoisseur of fine arts and antiques may need a very much larger income to achieve the same level of utility as someone less well educated; yet it would be hard to justify a substantial difference in their incomes on these grounds alone. Or, to take a rather different kind of case, consider a misanthrope with a determinedly miserable outlook on life and compare him with an optimist who remains happy and cheerful, despite encountering the most dreadful adversities: a Scrooge and a Tiny Tim. Should Scrooge receive a larger income in order to bring up his utility to that of Tiny Tim? It would be hard to describe such an outcome as fair.

I shall return to the question of the status of preferences in the next chapter. Here I want to draw attention to a rather different problem: one that concerns the way in which a particular distribution of utilities came about. For instance, suppose an individual tried unsuccessfully to steal another's handbag, but got hurt in the ensuing fracas. Should resources be transferred from the victim to the would-be criminal in order to equalize their utilities? To take another example, suppose there are two students with the same education, skills and family background, one of whom works hard for her final exams while the other spends most of his time playing poker. When the final exam results are announced, the hard worker, not surprisingly, does well and is pleased; the idler does badly and feels dissatisfied with himself and his performance. Their utilities are clearly unequal; yet it is hard to see that there is much unfairness in this situation.

The central point that is being made here is this. In general, we cannot simply observe inequality in either incomes or utilities and thereby judge, *on the basis of that inequality alone*, whether the distribution concerned is inequitable or not. We need to have more information: information about the circumstances in which those distributions arose. Equality of outcome will sometimes be equitable and sometimes not, depending on those circumstances. Precisely which bits of information concerning which circumstances are relevant to the equity judgement is a question that I address in the next chapter.

Envy-free allocations

Another interpretation of equity that has also recently received considerable attention in the economics literature is one that defines an equitable allocation as one that is *envy-free*: that is, if no individual prefers any other individual's allocation to his or her own. It was first put forward in this form by Foley (1967) and was developed by Kolm (1972), Varian (1974, 1975), Pazner and Schmeidler (1974) and others in the mid-1970s. Since then the literature has expanded considerably, culminating in a book by Baumol (1986), which also provides a brief history of the development of the idea (ch. 3, Appendix).

Although Foley is credited by Varian as being the originator of the idea, it has its origins in the older conception of 'how to cut a cake fairly'. If a cake is to be divided between two people, then a 'fair' method of doing so is for one to cut the cake and for the other to choose her portion. The resulting allocation should be acceptable to both, envy-free and therefore equitable (Dubins and Spanier 1961).

It might be thought that in promoting a 'new' idea of equity the first concern would be to establish its acceptability by, for instance, direct reference to intuition, or by using impartiality mechanisms such as a Rawlsian social contract discussed in the previous chapter. But, on the whole, this has not been the principal concern of these writers. Varian (1975) for example, argues that the definition 'is of interest in formalizing certain ordinary concepts of equity' (p. 240). But, as Sugden (1984) points out, 'what follows is not a moral argument, nor an analysis of how people ordinarily use the concept of equity. It is a technical argument, designed to show that this concept of fairness is quite operational' (pp. 506–7). The book by Baumol (1986), the most sustained treatment of the concept, devotes one page out of 266 to the idea's philosophical underpinnings; and this simply points to the difficulties of trying to obtain an agreed definition of equity given the variety of ways in which 'the term is used in common parlance' (p. 11).[3]

Instead, the principal concern of most of these writers is with the equity–efficiency trade-off; or, more precisely, with the trade-off between this conception of equity and efficiency defined as Pareto-optimality. Batteries of intellectual artillery are deployed to establish the conditions under which allocations exist that are simultaneously equitable (under this definition) and Pareto-optimal – allocations that, as noted in Chapter 2, are termed 'fair' in much of this literature, thus conflating fairness with Pareto-optimality and displaying a disregard for the English language that may be symptomatic of a lack of a philosophical base for the ideas.

A significant aspect of this literature is that, if no 'fair' allocations are found to exist under certain 'realistic' conditions, then the definition of envy-freeness – indeed of envy itself – is altered in order to ensure that some do exist. For example, one of the early results to be established was that, in economies with production, it may be impossible to find allocations that are simultaneously envy-free and Pareto-optimal (Pazner and Schmeidler 1974). Accordingly, several alternative definitions of envy were suggested, for which such allocations do exist. For instance, it was proposed that envy does not exist (and hence an allocation is equitable) if an individual prefers her own consumption and work effort to the consumption of any other individual *and* the work effort that it would be necessary for her to have to make in order to produce as much as the other (Varian 1974). Since differences in necessary work effort depend on people's income-earning abilities, in effect this is saying that no-one 'envies' another's superior abilities: a statement that seems factually incorrect, as well as having little apparent connection with intuitive or other interpretations of equity.

Another example of a concept developed in response to the difficulties of finding distributions that were simultaneously envy-free and Pareto-optimal is the suggestion that an allocation be defined as equitable if its distribution of utilities could have been achieved by an equal division of any set of commodities (Pazner and Schmeidler 1978). Again, the principal argument put forward to justify this definition is that it permits 'fair' (equitable and Pareto-optimal) allocations to exist. Again, no moral justification is offered;

indeed it is hard to see what it would have been. Yet another example is given by Archibald and Donaldson (1979), who define equity in terms of equality of choices but who do not provide anything by way of moral argument to support their definition; the omission here is even more striking, because, as will be argued in subsequent chapters, a strong case can be made for this interpretation in terms of moral acceptability.

The rationale is not immediately apparent for this emphasis on the importance of finding a definition of equity such that feasible allocations exist which are simultaneously equitable and efficient. In a pluralistic world, it seems quite plausible to suppose that there may be objectives whose simultaneous achievement is impossible. Economists, in particular, should be sympathetic to the possibility of trade-offs between objectives – in other contexts, after all, the trade-off is the hallmark of the profession. There seems to be nothing intrinsic in the concept of equity (or indeed of any other moral value) which requires that, for a particular conception to be acceptable, feasible allocations must exist that are simultaneously equitable and Pareto-optimal; to use this property to justify a particular conception of equity regardless of the latter's intuitive basis seems an unsatisfactory order of priority.

But is it possible to make an intuitive case for the concept? It will appeal to those who believe that a concern for equity springs from envy. If the mainspring of that concern is envy, then the absence of envy should eliminate the concern. In these circumstances, no one will worry about injustice or inequity in a society that is envy-free; that society, by implication, will therefore be equitable. It has also been argued (by, for example, Baumol 1986, p. 6) that a further advantage of the approach is that the decision on whether a distribution is equitable or not depends only on the wants or preferences of the individuals concerned; there is no need to import the analyst's values concerning equity, except in the fundamental sense that she must believe that all that matters in determining the desirability or otherwise of distributions are individual preferences.

Sugden (1984) has pointed out that there is an inconsistency in the belief that nothing matters except the satisfaction of preferences and the belief that envy-freeness is good. But there is a more fundamental objection to the idea. Chapter 2 discussed the notion that the concerns of equity sprang solely from considerations of envy, and concluded that they did not. That being the case, it is not surprising that the envy-free interpretation of the term does not always conform to the way in which it is generally used. It is quite possible to conceive of situations, which we might consider to be equitable, but where envy persists, or, alternatively situations where there is no envy, but which nonetheless might be considered as inequitable. For an example of the first, consider two brothers, sons of a rich parent, who divide the estate between them on their parent's death. Suppose that both are well-informed, rational individuals, identical in all respects, except in terms of their preferences for present and future consumption: their rates of time preference. One has a high rate of time preference and chooses to spend his inheritance immediately on expensive items of luxury consumption; the other, with a lower rate of time preference, prefers to invest his share and live off the income. After the prodigal's portion of the inheritance has all been spent, he becomes very poor; and in his penurious situation he envies his still wealthy brother. According to the envy-free definition of equity, such a situation is inequitable; on those grounds, the prodigal has a legitimate claim on his brother's wealth. But would this really be fair? If the prodigal was starving, we might argue that his brother should take him in or help him in some other way; but the claim here would be one of compassion, not because such an action would be fair or equitable.

An example of a situation where no envy exists but that

might nonetheless be regarded as inequitable is a caste society with great inequality in power and privilege, but in which the privileged had ensured by careful propaganda that those at the bottom knew their place and were content with it. A similar situation is that of the 'happy slave'; we are unlikely to regard slavery as a fair system, even if we were genuinely convinced that all slaves were happy with their situation.

Problems of this kind also arise with the 'envy-free' method of allocating the cake. Suppose that one of the two individuals concerned had baked the cake; might not she have a claim, on equity grounds, to a larger share? Or suppose there was an imbalance of knowledge between the cutter and the chooser: the former knew that some parts of it were more nutritious than other parts. In both these situations, it seems unsatisfactory to judge the allocation that resulted as equitable.

As these examples illustrate, the fundamental problem with this conception is that the absence of envy is neither a sufficient nor a necessary condition for an allocation to be judged equitable, at least as the term is conventionally used. In most cases, these judgements seem to require more information about the underlying situation than simply the absence or presence of envy. Equity cannot be adequately characterized by envy-freeness.

Horizontal equity and rank reversals

The concepts of horizontal and vertical equity are generally discussed in the literature on the economics of taxation (Musgrave 1959, 1976). Horizontal equity in tax policy requires that equals should be treated equally, and vertical equity that unequals should be treated unequally.

Now these may meet the criterion of general intuitive acceptability; for it is difficult to imagine anyone taking issue with these requirements as they stand. But they do so at the expense of specificity. Precisely who are equal and who unequal? What is meant by treatment? What form should the different treatment of unequals take? These principles cannot be applied in any meaningful way until these questions are answered; but, as soon as any attempt is made to do so, consensus is likely to disappear. In fact, in this form all the concepts embody is 'the formal principle of all moralities which are not actually anti-rational: don't act capriciously' (Watkins, quoted in Rees 1971).

However, there have been recent attempts to give horizontal equity, in particular, more content. This is the identification of horizontal inequity with the absence of 'rank reversals', an idea that has attracted attention from several distinguished economists (see, for example, Atkinson 1980; Feldstein 1976; M. King 1983a; Plotnick 1981, 1982, 1985). Under this interpretation, a tax change that affects the distribution of income or utility between individuals is identified as horizontally equitable if, despite the change, individuals' rankings in the initial distribution are preserved; it is horizontally inequitable if it causes individuals' positions in the distribution to change. So, for example, a tax change that demoted one individual from the top of the income distribution to the bottom would be inequitable; so would a less dramatic change, such as one reversing the rankings of two individuals next to each other in the distribution. An advantage of the interpretation is that the extent of inequity can be measured by the number of rank changes.

The rationale for this identification of horizontal inequity with rank reversals is rarely spelt out, but seems to be something like the following example (Plotnick 1985, p. 242). Suppose the initial distribution were regarded as fair or equitable (presumably according to some other different notion of equity). Everyone within the distribution would be equal in the sense that they are receiving what they 'ought' to receive. Then the ranking that was part of that distribution would also obviously be equitable. Hence, any policy that altered the rankings would be treating equals unequally; it would therefore be horizontally inequitable.

The idea has not been without its critics. Berliant and Strauss (1985), for example, provide two counter-examples. The first is as follows. Suppose all individuals are members of just two income groups, one with a high mean income and one with a low mean income. Suppose, further, that each individual has her group's mean income. Now a tax change is introduced that treats individuals in each group identically *but* reverses the income ordering of the groups. In this case there would be a considerable number of rank reversals; and, therefore, according to this interpretation of the term, a considerable amount of horizontal inequity. But, argue Berliant and Strauss, the tax change would in fact be horizontally equitable because it treated equals (that is, each group member) equally.

The idea that horizontal equity is best interpreted with reference to the treatment of individuals within specific groups is an important one, and is developed by Jenkins (1988).[4] But its use here does not have the power that Berliant and Strauss believe. If the initial income distribution were fair – as has to be assumed from the rank reversals' measure – then the initial ranking of the two groups was also fair. All individuals, regardless of which group they belong to, are therefore 'equal' in the sense that they are being fairly treated in the initial income distribution. To create a group reversal of the kind postulated, the redistributive policy would *not* be treating equals equally, for the members in one group are being treated differently from members of the other group. Therefore, the policy is indeed horizontally inequitable.

A more telling criticism might be the following. For an initial income distribution to be fair, presumably not only would the ordinal rankings be fair but so would the cardinal ordering. Hence, any policy that altered the cardinal gaps between incomes would create inequity. But this would not be captured by this definition. To take the Berliant and Strauss example: suppose the tax policy did not reverse the rankings of the groups but instead simply narrowed the income difference between them. If the income distribution were initially equitable – and if the cardinal gap between the groups were therefore regarded as equitable – the new distribution would be inequitable. Equals would not have been treated equally and horizontal equity violated, even though there had been no rank reversal.

Berliant and Strauss's second example relates to this point. Suppose all individuals are concentrated in a narrow range of incomes. A tax-and-transfer system is introduced that takes income from those at the bottom of the income distribution and gives it to those at the top. It thus widens the gap between those at the top of the income distribution and those at the bottom, but without altering the ordering. According to the no-rank-reversal interpretation of equity this does not violate horizontal equity; this despite the fact that some 'equals' have received hand-outs while others experience losses.

But perhaps the most fundamental objection to this procedure concerns the assumption that the original distribution is equitable, so that everyone in the initial distribution is – in an equity relevant sense – equal. Surely the aim of most of the tax-transfer policies whose horizontal inequity is being assessed is precisely to correct some at least of the inequities in the original income distribution? In that case, it is perfectly possible that some rank reversals may be equitable; and in which case the extent to which rank reversals occur may be an indication of a policy's *success* in equity terms, rather than an indication of its failure (Jenkins 1988).

It is only fair to point out that some of those who use this interpretation are not unaware of the problems associated with it. Plotnick (1985), for example, says in a footnote: 'If one wants to label rank-order requirements something other than horizontal inequity, so be it. Semantics aside, my interest in this study is in understanding and quantifying the extent of such reversals' (p. 241). But definitions of equity are not just matters of semantics; they relate to fundamental questions of value. Further, if a concern for equity does *not* underlie the issue of rank reversals, then what does? The lacuna of any other justification is recognized by Plotnick, for he legitimizes his study of rank reversals throughout the rest of his paper by continuous identification with horizontal inequity. Yet, as we have seen, such an identification needs much more justification than it has been given.

Although the principal focus of this literature is on horizontal equity, it is often accompanied by an interpretation of vertical equity that identifies it with income equality (see, for example, Plotnick 1985, p. 244). We have already discussed the difficulties of this interpretation, but it might be noted here that there is a fundamental contradiction between vertical equity defined in terms of income inequality and horizontal equity defined in terms of rank reversals. For the former assumes that, so long as it is unequal, the initial income distribution is inequitable, while the latter, as we have seen, assumes that it is not. Despite these interpretations often appearing next to one another, they are not mutually consistent.

Utilitarianism

Let us now turn to a more comprehensive system, one that has had an enormous influence on economics in general and on economic approaches to equity in particular: utilitarianism.[5] There are two possible ways in which utilitarianism can be linked with equity. First, equity may be *defined* in utilitarian terms. That is, an allocation is defined as equitable if it is the outcome of a specific application of utilitarian principles. Alternatively, the link may arise because, under certain specific circumstances, utilitarian allocations are egalitarian in outcome. Unfortunately, as several writers have shown, neither position is convincing.

It is simple to find situations where utilitarian allocations are unlikely to be either equal or equitable. Sen (1973), for instance, gives the example of two individuals, one healthy and one physically disabled. The physically disabled person, because of her handicap, finds it more difficult to 'generate' utility from her income than does the healthy individual; that is, each pound's worth of income is worth less to her. A utilitarian redistribution of income from a starting position of equal incomes would require taking income away from the disabled person and giving it to the healthy individual. Hence, the distribution of income would become unequal – and, in many people's eyes, inequitable.

To take another example, consider a utilitarian distribution of education. This would require that education be allocated to those who derive most utility from it. Now it is well established that children from wealthy backgrounds derive more benefit from a given amount of educational input than do the children of equal ability but from less advantaged homes. Hence, utilitarianism would imply that education should be concentrated on the former rather than the latter. Again an inegalitarian outcome; and again one that many would consider as inequitable.

It is true that under certain conditions utilitarian allocations are equal ones. For instance, if there were two individuals who derived the same utility from a given level of income (that is, if they had identical utility functions) and if the utility from an extra pound's worth of income decreased as income increased (that is, if there were diminishing marginal utility of income), then a utilitarian distribution of income would be an equal one. For, if it were not, it would always be possible to increase the sum of utilities by taking away income from the richer of the two individuals and giving it to the poorer. However, even if equality of incomes were regarded as equitable (and we have already seen a number of reasons why it might not be so regarded), this would not imply that utilitarianism itself was equitable. The egalitarian outcome in this situation is a fluke. It is dependent on a variety of assumptions, especially those of identical utility functions and diminishing marginal utility of income. If either of these assumptions is not met, utilitarianism can lead to quite inegalitarian outcomes – as was demonstrated in the handicap and education examples (where the assumption of identical utility functions was violated).

Thus utilitarianism does not necessarily generate outcomes that are either equitable or equal. Nor is this surprising. The focus of utilitarianism is on maximizing the sum of individual utilities; hence, as Sen (1973, p. 16) puts it 'it is supremely unconcerned with the interpersonal distribution of the sum'. In Barry's terminology, it is an *aggregative* not a *distributive* principle (Barry 1965, ch. 3). Since the principal focus of equity is on interpersonal distribution, utilitarianism is therefore unlikely to provide us with the interpretation that we seek.

Rawls and maximin

Rawls (1972) made two contributions to the debate concerning theories of justice: the use of the social contract as a means of establishing moral principles, and the argument that individuals drawing up a social contract in the 'initial position' would choose two particular principles of justice.

Some of the problems involved in using the social contract as a method of establishing the validity of moral principles in general were discussed in the previous chapter, and I shall not repeat the arguments here. But one, more specific, point should be made. This method of validating the principle is not concerned directly with equity. Rather, it is the predicted

outcome of the decisions that would be made by selfish individuals if they were in a specific hypothetical situation: that
of the initial position. These individuals are not concerned
with what would be equitable in the society whose prospec-
tive organization they are considering, but only with their
own interests in that society. Their concern for the least
advantaged expressed in Rawls' second principle, for
example, derives not from any basic notion that the least
advantaged suffer from inequity or injustice, but from a fear
that they themselves might turn out to be the least advantaged. No moral principles are being invoked here, only self-
interest.

Rawls gives several formulations of his two principles
of justice. The most authoritative ones seem to be the
following:

> Each person is to have an equal right to the most extensive
> total system of equal basic liberties compatible with a
> similar system of liberty for all (Rawls 1972, p. 250).

> Social and economic inequalities are to be arranged so that
> they are (a) to the greatest benefit of the least advantaged
> and (b) attached to offices and positions open to all under
> conditions of fair equality of opportunity. (Rawls 1972,
> p. 83)

These principles, and their method of derivation, have
been subject to considerable critical attention elsewhere (see,
for example, Wolff 1972; Barry 1973, 1989a; Daniels 1975;
Pettit 1980) and no full-scale critique will be attempted
here. Our concern is simply to judge the acceptability of the
definition of equity implicit in the principles.

Of these, the first, despite its label as a principle of
'justice', deals more with the requirements of individual
liberty than with those of equity, and hence has not figured

prominently in the literature with which we are concerned. However, the second, termed by Rawls the 'difference' principle and by others the 'maximin' principle, has played a major role in discussions of fairness or equity and therefore requires more extensive treatment.

Given that, as we saw above, the principle is actually derived by individuals pursuing their own self-interest, it is not surprising that, as Nozick says (1974, p. 204), 'the difference principle is on the face of it unfair'. A given distribution may be totally 'just' in a Rawlsian sense, but unjust or inequitable when judged by more conventional standards of justice or equity. For example, under the principle, individuals who have skills useful for raising the levels of the least advantaged, either because of a natural endowment or because they have acquired them through their family background, would be 'bribed' to exercise those skills; that is, they would receive rewards on the basis of their natural endowment or family background. A concrete instance of this is the use of incentive payments to encourage family practitioners to set up their surgeries in poor areas. Yet is it fair that one individual should receive more than another simply because she has a different natural endowment or family background? Rawls himself does not think so; he says at the beginning of his book that intuition requires a 'conception of justice that nullifies the accidents of natural endowment and of social circumstances' (Rawls 1972, p. 15). Yet, as the example shows, this is a condition that is not met by the maximin principle.

It should be noted that this argument does not invalidate the use of the maximin principle (or Rawls's other principle) as a social objective *independent* of equity or justice. Thus we might believe in the primacy of the aim of helping the least well-off and hence accept that a certain amount of inequity or injustice is necessary to achieve that aim. So, for example, we might not think it fair for doctors to receive large sums to induce them to devote their skills to helping the least well-off, but nonetheless accept a system that does reward them disproportionately for the sake of the less well-off themselves. In other words, we may be prepared to trade-off a measure of equity in favour of the maximin principle; but this is not the same as saying that the principle is itself equitable.

A related difficulty concerns the definition of the least well-off themselves. In the example given earlier of the idle and the hard-working student, the latter is likely to be better off in her subsequent career than the former; but is this unjust? In the similar case of the profligate individual who dissipated his inheritance, does he have a claim on the wealth of his wiser brother on the grounds that he is now the less well-off of the two?

Rawls does not seem to address directly the issues raised by examples such as this. He does use terms such as 'least-advantaged' and 'least fortunate' interchangeably with 'least well-off' throughout his book, thus perhaps implying that his concern is only for those among the less well-off who are in their plight because of misfortune; but he does not make any systematic distinction between them and those who are poor as a consequence of their own choices.

One line of defence that could be used against this argument, indeed one used by Rawls in his subsequent work, is that the maximin principle is not intended for use in individual cases of the kind discussed. Rather, it is a principle to be applied only to the organization of the wider society: it is a 'macro-criterion and not a micro-criterion' (Rawls 1974, p. 142). But this is not very compelling. As Nozick (1974, pp. 204–7) has pointed out, there seems no convincing reason for separating 'micro' from 'macro' situations. If a principle of justice is applicable to one, then why should it be inapplicable to the other? It is an odd principle whose applicability is determined by the scale of the situation whose equity is to be assessed.

In short, as with utilitarianism, the maximin principle does not really capture the essence of the term equity as it is conventionally used.

Non-equity principles of distribution

There are other principles that address the same issues as equity principles – particularly those concerned with distribution – but do not necessarily invoke considerations of equity or justice in their defence. Two of the more interesting of these are the principle of so-called 'Pareto-optimal redistribution', and an apparently similar distributional rule put forward by the libertarian, Robert Nozick. Although not derived from a concern with equity, their proponents have contrasted them favourably with equity principles as guides to distributional policy, and therefore they deserve some consideration here.

Nozick (1974) summarizes his rule as: 'from each as he chooses, to each as he is chosen' (p. 160). In the course of his argument leading up to its presentation, he states explicitly that he is not putting forward a theory of justice (p. 153); rather, the rule is simply a logical consequence of the lexicographical priority he gives to individual liberty. For Nozick, the requirements of liberty include the right to give away income (or anything else) as one chooses; but they also include the right not to give anything away, if one does not so choose.

In the light of the widely held view that Pareto-optimality is a definition of efficiency (a view challenged in Chapter 3), it may seem odd to treat it as a 'rival' to principles of distribution that derive from concerns of equity or justice. However, it is relatively simple to demonstrate the way in which it can be used as a guide to distributional questions. In the example used earlier (see p. 80), Amanda had a

higher income than Catherine, because of racial discrimination against the latter. Now suppose Amanda derives some
utility from an increase in Catherine's income. This could
happen for any of a number of reasons, including: Amanda
knows Catherine and cares about her welfare; Amanda does
not know Catherine but observes (and is distressed by) the
fact that Catherine is very poor; Amanda objects to racial discrimination; or Amanda feels that her wealth is threatened
by Catherine's poverty and believes the threat would be
reduced if Catherine were less poor.

Now suppose further that, at their current income levels,
Amanda would derive more utility or satisfaction from
transferring £1's worth of income to Catherine than she
would from spending it on herself. In that case, for the
transfer to take place would be a Pareto-improvement, since
both individuals would be better off in terms of their
utilities. Indeed, further transfers would also be Pareto-
improvements, until the point is reached where the utility
to Amanda of a marginal increase in Catherine's income
becomes less than the marginal utility to Amanda of her own
income. Beyond this point, further transfers would result in
a net drop in Amanda's utility and hence could not be
justified on Paretian grounds.

This kind of analysis could be used as a positive hypothesis
concerning redistribution. That is, it could be hypothesized
that an observed pattern of redistribution is actually the
result of a process similar to that described above and hence
that the redistribution is Pareto-optimal. It has indeed been
used this way to analyse a number of redistributive programmes: analyses that have in turn attracted much criticism
(Giertz 1982; Pasour 1981, 1983).

However, it is the use of Pareto-optimality as a normative
guide to redistribution, rather than as a tool of positive
analysis, that is of interest here. Several of the authors concerned have advocated that it be used in this way. Thus
Hochman and Rodgers (1969) argue: 'Our approach ...

implies that redistributive activities can be justified without a social welfare function that makes interpersonal comparisons' (p. 543). In addition, Giertz (1982) claims: 'With all of its limitations, the use of Pareto optimality as a (limited) guide to redistribution questions is infinitely superior to the approach often used of envoking [sic] a social welfare function. Distribution questions which cannot be resolved using the standard of Pareto optimality are ones for which there are no generally acceptable normative standards for making such decisions' (p. 281).

As was argued at the end of Chapter 4, the fact that the use of this approach obviates the need for interpersonal comparisons of utility seems of secondary importance. And it was pointed out in Chapter 3 that Pareto-optimality itself incorporates a 'normative standard' that is unlikely to be 'generally acceptable'.[6] However, there is a more fundamental difficulty with both this rule and that of Nozick. Both give primacy to the preferences of the person who 'loses' income in the redistribution process. If that person approves of redistribution away from herself, then the redistribution is desirable; if she does not approve, it is undesirable. For both rules, the preferences of anyone receiving income under the redistribution process do not count; nor do those of anyone else.[7]

And, of course, it is here that their weakness as a guide to redistribution policy lies, at least for anyone with a concern for equity or justice. Why should the extent of redistribution depend only on the preferences of those who will lose under the redistribution? They are hardly likely to be impartial. If they have no concern for the welfare of others, then there will be no redistribution. In our example, if Amanda had no interest of any kind in Catherine, then under both rules Catherine would remain poor – an outcome that is unlikely to be judged equitable, however equity is interpreted.

In short, rules of this kind cannot be regarded as 'infinitely superior' to equity or justice principles, simply because they do not address the fundamental issues of equity or justice. At the end of the day, because the rules are not based on any notion of equity, they are not likely to be equitable. This will not trouble those who do not believe that equity or justice has a place among the list of social values with which policy should be concerned; but, for those who do, it is an insuperable objection.

Conclusion

This chapter has attempted to assess the intuitive basis of judgements concerning the equity or otherwise of particular situations. To this end, a number of conceptions of equity have been examined. In summary form, they define a distribution of resources as equitable if:

- it has the outcome that income or utility are distributed equally;
- it is envy-free;
- it meets the requirements of horizontal and vertical equity;
- it is the outcome of maximizing the sum of individual utilities;
- it is the outcome of maximizing the position of the least well-off;
- it is Pareto-optimal, or the outcome of voluntary choices.

Of these, it was argued that none captures the essential element of the concept as it appears in general usage.

This fact – that it seems to be possible to find examples for each of the conceptions considered where their application would produce outcomes inconsistent with intuitive judgements of equity – suggests that there is some fundamental element in those judgements which is not being taken into account. The analysis of this chapter has gone some way towards finding out what this is. All the conceptions considered are what are commonly termed 'end-result' principles. That is, the equity or otherwise of a given distribution is determined by the structure of that distribution. However, the arguments here suggest our judgements concerning the equity of that situation will generally depend on how it came about. Simple observation of the fact that, say, two individuals have different incomes, is not sufficient to determine the equity of that situation. We need more information on *why* they had different incomes before we can make such a judgement. Precisely what information is relevant to that judgement will become apparent in the next chapter.

Notes: Chapter 5

1 As Broome has noted, 'Because the emphasis [of economists] is on proving theorems from assumptions, the assumptions are sometimes inadequately interpreted and justified, and some of them are foolish' (Broome 1989, p. 14). Broome himself is an important exception to this generalization: see Broome (forthcoming).
2 More recently, Sen has argued against the use of equality of utilities as a foundation for social justice; see, for example, Sen (1980).
3 To be fair (in a more usual interpretation of the term), some of the contributors to the literature have expressed moral reservations about this conception of equity: see, for example, Pazner (1975).
4 Specifically, Jenkins suggests that measures of re-ranking are confined to those that occur within groups.
5 See Broome (1989) for a description of the influence of utilitarianism on welfare economics.
6 The rule has been attacked on other, not wholly legitimate, grounds. For instance, Pasour (1983) accuses Giertz of arguing that Pareto-optimality provides a value-free basis for income redistribution, and criticizes this position by claiming that any assessment of other people's levels of utility involves a value-judgement. But this is confusing judgements of value with judgements of fact.
7 The two rules seem similar, but they are not in fact identical. For instance, the Nozickian rule explicitly forbids compulsory redistribution, whereas such redistribution can be justified by the Paretian rule under certain circumstances (for instance, if there is a free-rider effect).

6 Equity and choice

Consider some of the examples discussed in the previous chapter. There, distributions were considered inequitable if:

- some people had lower incomes than others because of their colour;
- an individual who robbed another was fully compensated for injuries sustained in the robbery;
- an idle student received the same examination result as a hard-working one;
- an individual who dissipated an inheritance was compensated;
- someone disabled from birth had a low income solely as a consequence of a physical handicap;
- children from poor families received less education than those from rich ones;
- an individual received a larger income than another simply because of an accident of birth or family circumstance.

What is the essential feature of these distributions that creates the apparent inequity? In each case it seems to be regarded as inequitable if individuals receive less than others because of factors *beyond their control*. The black, disabled, or poorly endowed individuals had no choice in determining their situation. Hence, any distribution that discriminates against them seems unfair. On the other hand, if people's situations were the outcome of their own choices (for example, the individual who chose to spend an inheritance instead of saving it, the idle student and the robber), then the distributions that result do not seem so inequitable. Distributions that are the outcome of factors beyond individual control are generally considered inequitable; distributions that are the outcome of individual choices are not.

The crucial element that was missing from some of the previous attempts to define equity thus appears to be its relationship to the existence of choice. For the examples considered suggest that *our judgements concerning the degree of inequity inherent in a given distribution depend on the extent to which we see that distribution as the outcome of individual choice*. If one individual receives less than another owing to her own choice, then the disparity is not considered inequitable; if it arises for reasons beyond her control, then it is inequitable.

Equality of choices

This idea can be expressed more formally as follows. Define the factors beyond individual control as *constraints*. These constraints limit the range of possibilities over which individuals can make their choices. Define the set of possibilities bounded by the constraints as the *choice set*. Then, *a distribution is equitable if it is the outcome of informed individuals choosing over equal choice sets*.

This interpretation is now attracting attention from both economists and political philosophers.[1] It seems to have a number of advantages over those discussed in the previous chapter. The most obvious is that which forms the basis of its derivation: that it captures common usage more effectively. As a further illustration of this, consider the ideas of need and desert which, as we noted in Chapter 4, underlie many common perceptions of equity, but which have not been adequately recognized in the conceptions previously considered. This conception obviously corresponds to at least one interpretation of desert: that people 'deserve' to bear the consequences of their own choices, provided that the range of choices they had open to them were much the same as everyone else's. But, perhaps less obviously, it can also be viewed as capturing some of the reasons why distribution according to need is often considered equitable. One interpretation of the statement that someone needs X to do Y is that, if Y is to happen, the person concerned has no choice but to have X. Thus to state that human beings need food to survive is to say that human beings have no choice but to have food if they are to survive. More generally, distribution according to need can be viewed as compensating people for elements critical to survival that are *beyond their control*: the fact that to survive, they need food, shelter, warmth, etc.

A further illustration of the ability of the conception to reflect common usage concerns the reaction of many non-economists to some economists' policy prescriptions. Rent control and minimum wage legislation are classic illustrations of policies where the views of economists (who generally oppose them) differ from those held by large sections of the population. The difference is doubtless partly because the efficiency costs of such policies are not as widely known as they should be; but it is also reasonable to suppose that many people regard high rents and low wages as unfair because those who have to suffer them often have little control over their situation.

Similar examples are discussed by Baumol (1986, pp. 1–2). For instance, a survey in the United Kingdom comparing the views of economists and MPs found a striking divergence of views between the two groups concerning the use of peak-period surcharges for commuters, with the economists supporting it and a majority of MPs of both political persuasions opposing it. The MPs were apparently less concerned with any efficiency advantages that might flow from this pricing policy than with their belief that commuters were a captive market, with little choice about paying the surcharge.

Another example mentioned by Baumol concerns the application of the Ramsey theorem concerning the pricing policy of public utilities. This suggests that, under conditions of increasing returns to scale, if it is necessary to cover costs, then prices of products with inelastic demands should be raised above marginal costs. But in a court decision that dealt with the issue, the judge felt that such an outcome was unfair, because the burden was thereby placed on people who could go nowhere else, whose demands were inelastic because they had little choice.

Doubtless the difference between economists' and others' views of these situations arises partly because of differences in their perceptions of the actual choices that people are perceived to have in the relevant situations. However, this simply illustrates that it may be possible to agree upon this definition of equity, but to disagree upon its application in different situations. For example, consider two opposing political views concerning those in poverty; a 'Rightist' view that they should receive little help, since they have presumably chosen not to avail themselves of the opportunities for making money in our society; and a 'Leftist' view that the poor are proper recipients of aid, since they are 'locked into' poverty through a variety of social and economic impediments to social mobility. Now both Rightist and Leftist could accept our definition of equity: that, to the extent the poor's income is the result of the constraints they face, then inequity exists. The disagreement would arise over precisely what factors constituted constraints and what did not. The discussion between them, therefore, would have shifted from a value plane to an empirical one: the extent to which the individuals' decisions which led to the distributions concerned were or were not constrained.

It could be objected in this line of argument, that the shift of the debate from 'values' to 'facts' does not constitute a great improvement. There may be just as many arguments concerning the extent to which differences in individual incomes arise from differences in constraints, as there are value-judgements about equity.

To this there are two responses. First, even if the argument does not resolve whether a particular distribution is equitable or not, it is important to clarify what the battle is about. A disagreement concerning values is different from one concerning the extent of individual choice, and it is necessary to be clear which is being discussed. Secondly, even if it is accepted that it will be difficult to obtain consensus on *all* the factors which may constitute constraints, it is likely that agreement can be reached on *some* of them. For example, most people would agree that the amount an individual may inherit is generally beyond his or her control. It should be possible, therefore, to obtain agreement that a given distribution is inequitable, even if it is impossible to decide what would constitute one that was fully equitable. Illustrations of how such judgements can be made in specific cases can be found in subsequent chapters.

The definition also has the advantage of meeting some of the alternative criteria for acceptability mentioned at the end of Chapter 4. These concerned its comprehensibility and its information requirements. The definition is easily comprehensible. So far as information requirements are concerned, there are difficulties in measuring choice sets, as we shall see in Chapter 9; but the requirements seem low in comparison to most of the other definitions considered. In particular, no interpersonal utility comparisons or assumptions concerning cardinal utility functions are necessary.

So far, we have discussed the advantages of the conception. One disadvantage is that it may not be complete. It is possible there may be some distributions that arise from decisions taken over different choice sets but that nonetheless an observer may judge as equitable. For instance, it could be considered that an individual whose choices did not include certain possibilities might be 'compensated' by the extension of her choices to include different items. For instance the ability of an intelligent but disabled individual to obtain professional training and thereby increase her income could be viewed as compensation for her inability to participate in extensive physical activity.

However, it is difficult to include considerations such as this in any universal conception of equity. What seems to be happening in such judgements is that the observer making the judgement is imposing her own preferences upon the choices concerned, and inferring that, if she were confronted with either set, the items she would choose would yield her the same level of satisfaction. Since doubtless different observers have different views on what items would adequately compensate individuals for the absence of other items, it seems unlikely that any general consensus would be found on whether different choice sets were 'equivalent' or not. Accordingly, it seems preferable to use the conception of equal choice sets as the basic definition of equity, but with the acknowledgement that there may be distributions of choices which do not meet the criterion of full equality, but which some observers might nonetheless consider equitable.

There are several other points that merit deeper discussion. These are the relationship between the concept and that of the apparently similar ideas of equality of opportunity and equality of resources; the status of preferences; and the role of chance.

Equality of opportunity and equality of resources

The idea that equity requires equality of choice sets is obviously akin to the notion that equity requires equality of opportunity. However, it is in fact rather broader than

equality of opportunity, at least as the latter is conventionally used, and it is worth spelling out why.

The attainment of equality of opportunity is usually taken
to mean the removal of economic and social barriers to the
fulfilment of individual potential. Thus, there is inequality
of opportunity if a bright student from a poor family cannot
continue her studies because of the cost of college fees, or if
a black candidate for promotion is denied it because of racial
prejudice. In these situations, equality of opportunity will be
achieved if fees are waived for poor students, or if discrimination on the grounds of race is outlawed (and if the laws are
properly enforced).

It is clear that the cost of college fees, or the existence of
racial discrimination, are factors beyond individual control
and, hence, according to this definition, possible sources of
inequity. However, it does not follow that simply removing
barriers such as these will ensure equality of choice sets and
therefore equity. Even if college fees are waived, bright
students from poor families may have to stop their studies
because they need to earn money to support their families;
even if there is no organizational discrimination, black candidates for promotion may be disadvantaged because, having
been brought up in a racially divided society, they have not
acquired some of the confidence or skills of white candidates
and hence perform less well in the selection procedures.
In these cases, equality of choice sets may require positive
discrimination, with poorer students receiving larger grants
than students from well-off backgrounds, or with different
criteria being applied to black candidates for promotion.
Here equity, in the sense of equality of choice sets,
requires *in*equality of opportunity, in the sense of (positive)
discrimination.

In short, the conception has more radical implications
than a narrow interpretation of equality of opportunity.
Individuals' choice sets are determined not only by the social
and economic barriers they face but by their initial resources

or endowments, which include their natural abilities and the resources that they acquire through inheritance, gifts, family background, education prior to the age of majority, etc. Equalization of choice sets thus may require judicious manipulation of economic and other barriers in order to advantage the less well endowed. Or it may require compensating those with little natural ability by other resources, such as education, so as to bring their range of choices as close as possible to those naturally endowed.

That inequalities in resources (or, more strictly, in initial endowments) are sources of inequity seems to be an inevitable consequence of the arguments made earlier concerning the inequity of distributions that, for instance, discriminate against those with a physical handicap. And as such it has been endorsed by some important recent contributions to the philosophical literature.[2] However, equality of resources is not quite the same as equality of choices. It is possible for individuals to have the same resources and yet, because of factors beyond their control, not to have equality of choices. This may arise, for example, if some preferences are regarded as beyond individual control; and to this we now turn.

The status of preferences

Individuals' choices are affected not only by their resources but by their values, beliefs and tastes: by what may be termed their preferences. Implicit in much of the argument so far has been the assumption that these preferences are not among the factors that are considered as being beyond individual control. All preferences are regarded as autonomous. However, this assumption can create problems for the conception of equity as choice.

This can be illustrated by the following example. Suppose there are two individuals, one of whom likes oranges but hates apples while the other detests oranges but is rather partial to the occasional apple. Each is given a bowl of fruit that, because of factors beyond either's control, contains the same number of apples, but no oranges. Both people have equal choices; but nonetheless the orange-lover might regard the outcome as inequitable. She did not 'choose' to have a preference for oranges; yet, as a consequence of that preference, she will be less satisfied with the gift than the apple-lover.

Or consider a less trivial case. An accountant and a social worker are equally able, come from similar family backgrounds and have similar skills and education. However, the accountant greatly enjoys working with financial matters, whereas the social worker prefers dealing with people and their problems. Because of the way society is currently organized, the range of jobs that meet the accountant's preferences are better paid than those that meet the social worker's. Hence, although they have equal choice sets, the consequence of their exercising their respective preferences over those choice sets is likely to be that the accountant will have a much higher lifetime income than the social worker: an outcome that the social worker, or indeed anybody else, might not consider particularly equitable.

There is a general argument here concerning the status of preferences. Some might claim that all preferences are as much beyond individuals' control as their initial endowments. Attitudes, values, preferences for dealing with people instead of numbers, even the taste for apples and oranges, are the product of factors beyond individual control, such as family upbringing, education, biology and so on. Hence, even in a world of equal endowments, there would be outcomes that are beyond individual control, and therefore inequitable.

Now the first point to make is that, even if preferences are beyond individual control, this does not create difficulties for the principle that underlies our definition: that inequity is present in distributions where people are disadvantaged owing to factors beyond their control. If some people are disadvantaged solely because of their preferences and if it can be established incontrovertibly that these preferences were beyond their control, then their situation is indeed inequitable. There is no clash here between intuition and the conception of equity as choice. As Cohen (1989) argues, *the relevant distinction for equity purposes is not between preferences and resources, but between factors that are beyond an individual's control and those that are not.*[3]

But are all preferences beyond individual control? To believe that all preferences are predetermined implies that people actually have no choice in what they do and therefore that there is no free will. This is a completely determinist position that few nowadays would find acceptable.

Alternatively, it could be argued that some preferences are socially or otherwise determined, but others are not. People do have free will and they can make choices; but in practice some of their preferences are predetermined and therefore their actual choices are more constrained than a simple observation of the overt constraints that they face would suggest. But where should the line be drawn between those preferences that are predetermined and those that are not? If someone born into a rich family argues that, because of their family upbringing, they have very expensive tastes and therefore they 'need' to have a higher income than anyone else, is this an acceptable reason (in terms of equity) for them actually to receive a higher income? Do wine connoisseurs have an equity claim for a higher income than those content with cheap wine, so that they can indulge their expensive tastes?

In some cases it may be quite easy to draw the line. Take the example of wine connoisseurs who originally found cheap wine perfectly acceptable but have worked at developing their taste. In that case it seems reasonable to say that they have 'chosen' to acquire this particular preference, and it should not then be taken into account in making equity

judgements about their situation (Cohen, 1989). Preferences
that are themselves the consequence of choice are not sources
of inequity.

But this would still leave cases where people have not
'chosen' to have a particular preference but are nonetheless
disadvantaged by it. Barry (1990) has suggested a way out of
this dilemma. That is to ask whether someone is 'satisfied'
with their preferences, with the implication that if they are
satisfied we need not take those preferences into account
when making equity judgements. This suggestion is effectively one of trying to ascertain, not whether people had
actually chosen their preferences, but whether, if they had
been allowed to choose them, they would have chosen the
ones they have got. If, for some or all of their preferences,
the answer is yes, then we treat these preferences as autonomous or as though they were within their control; if the
answer is no, then we regard the preferences concerned as
beyond individual control and hence judge any differences
in outcome that directly result from the exercise of those
preferences as inequitable.

But this suggestion also has its difficulties. For instance, it
could be argued that it simply pushes the problem back a
level. What is the status of the factors that determine
whether people are satisfied or dissatisfied with their
preferences? Are they to be regarded as within or beyond
individual control? We could apply the same procedure at
this second level and ask whether the individual is satisfied
or dissatisfied with being the kind of person who is satisfied
or dissatisfied with their preferences; but then the same issue
would arise about the status of the factors that determine the
response to *that* question. There is clearly the danger here of
an infinite regress, which is likely to be ultimately
unprofitable both in philosophical and practical terms.

Perhaps the resolution of this issue lies in the concept of
the 'individual' who is making the choices. For what makes
a person individual if not her values, beliefs and tastes? Not

only does the concept of choice have no meaning if everything is predetermined, but it makes no sense unless there is someone to do the choosing. And it is difficult to see how that someone could be defined independently, at some level, of her preferences.

I say 'at some level', for to take the position that individuals 'are' their preferences does not necessarily preclude the possibility that some people may be dissatisfied with some of their preferences in the manner suggested by Barry (1990). It does not seem unreasonable to describe this situation as one where they are dissatisfied with themselves – or at least an aspect of themselves. But, if that description is acceptable, it reinforces the point that people can be identified with their preferences.

Overall, the question of the status of preferences is a part of the general debate concerning the extent of free will, a debate that has exercised the minds of many of the world's greatest philosophers and is not likely to be resolved here. At the end of the day, the solution for policy purposes probably has to be a pragmatic, case-by-case approach which focuses primarily on the role of outside constraints in creating equitable or inequitable situations, but which accepts that there are going to be occasions where preferences can be regarded as beyond individual control and therefore have to be taken into account. The next chapter provides an illustration of how this might be applied to a specific distributional situation: that of health care.

Chance

At first sight it might appear that the conception can deal with the role of chance or luck with little difficulty. Chance is, by definition, beyond individual control; therefore, any difference between people's situations that arise from chance are beyond their control and therefore inequitable.

However, as Barry (1990) has pointed out, this is not the end of the matter. Suppose two individuals purchase tickets in a lottery, and one wins. The winner's reward is the outcome of luck and therefore a consequence of a factor beyond her control. Therefore, it might appear that, according to the conception of equity as choice, on equity grounds her winnings should be redistributed to the loser (and indeed to anyone else who lost): an implication that seems neither very sensible nor very fair.

In reply to this it could be argued that the equity judgement should be applied not to the *ex post* situation after the outcome of the lottery but to the *ex ante* situation when the lottery ticket was purchased. If both individuals faced equal choice sets, both were fully informed about the lottery odds and the price of the lottery ticket was the same, then the eventual outcome could be regarded as a consequence of the choices made and therefore judged as equitable.

To reinforce the point, consider a less trivial example, similar to that used by Barry (1990). Suppose the economic situation is such that there is a measurable risk of involuntary long-term unemployment, say five per cent. Suppose further that this is a risk known to everyone and that it is the same for everyone; also, to simplify matters, assume that everyone does the same job (when in employment) and receives the same income.

Now, to help alleviate the economic distress that the unemployment causes, the state offers an unemployment insurance scheme into which people may voluntarily contract on the payment of a given premium. If they join the scheme they will receive full compensation for any income loss if they become unemployed. Given the offer, some join the scheme; some do not. Five per cent of those who join become unemployed, but, because the insurance scheme pays out, they suffer no loss of income. Five per cent of those who did not join the scheme also become unemployed; but, with no income, they come close to starvation.

Now the same argument used to justify the lottery outcome could be used to argue that people who become unemployed but who have failed to contract into the state insurance scheme have no claim on equity grounds for being compensated. By not joining the scheme, they voluntarily took a risk; and they lost. Their consequent distress might be such that they might have a claim to receive some help on compassionate grounds; but as noted in Chapter 2 allocations according to compassion are not the same as those according to equity.

However, this does not seem quite correct. In this situation, not every non-joiner will become unemployed; indeed, 95 per cent will not. The five per cent who do are the victims not solely of their own choices, but, at least in one sense, of bad luck. Hence, their situation is in large part an outcome of factors beyond their control.

One way of resolving these issues is to invoke the economist's conception of 'expected value'. The expected value of an uncertain outcome is the value of the outcome itself multiplied by the probability of the outcome actually occurring. So, for instance, the expected value of a lottery that offers a one in a hundred chance of winning £1,000 is one hundredth of £1,000 or £10. In the case we are considering, if the losses involved in being unemployed can be valued at, say, £10,000, the expected value of the loss due to being unemployed is five per cent of £10,000 or £500.

Now it seems reasonable to hold people responsible for the expected value of an uncertain outcome, *whether or not* the outcome actually occurs. In the situation described in our example, this could be achieved by compelling all individuals to join the state insurance scheme and charging a premium equal to the expected value. In that case, everyone would simply bear the financial cost of being unemployed, not only the five per cent unemployed themselves: an outcome that seems fair, given the fact that the unemployment is involuntary.

This way of resolving equity dilemmas concerning chance and choice seems to have considerable potential.[4] In the next chapter, this potential is illustrated, and the idea itself further developed, in relation to an area of uncertainty that affects everyone's lives: their state of health.

Conclusion

This chapter has argued that the concept of equity is intimately related to the existence or otherwise of choice. If people's choices are constrained, whether because of their lack of resources, or because of preferences that are beyond their control, this is likely to create inequity. The element that was missing from the conceptions of equity discussed in earlier chapters is any consideration of the extent of individual choice in determining the situations whose equity is to be judged; for it is that consideration which provides the core of consistency in the way the term is commonly used.

Finally, let me emphasize two points. First, to argue that choice matters in determining equity does not imply a belief about the extent of choice that people actually face in the real world. To return to an earlier example, a Rightist and a Leftist may both subscribe to the idea that differences in incomes that arise from differences in people's choices are not inequitable. But the Rightist believes that in practice people have much the same range of income-earning possibilities open to them and, therefore, that most income differences are not in fact inequitable, while the Leftist believes that in practice most people face very restricted choices, and hence that most earnings differences arise from factors beyond individual control and are therefore in fact inequitable. Both Rightist and Leftist are, in Barry's (1990) terminology, 'choicists'; the difference between them lies in their empirical judgement concerning the actual determinants of income differences. To accept the argument that there is a strong relationship between equity and choice does not imply accepting any particular view concerning the extent of the choices that people actually face; the relationship between equity and choice is a matter of value, the extent of choice a matter of fact.

The second point to be emphasized, or rather re-emphasized because it was discussed in Chapter 2, is the following: if equity requires equality of choices, then this does not imply that achieving full equality of choices should be the sole, or even the overriding aim, of policy. In many cases, perhaps most, it will be impossible to achieve full equality of choices without doing violence to other important values. For example, if inheritance is regarded as being beyond individual control and are therefore in fact inequitable. Both Rightist and Leftist are, in Barry's (1990) termin- from the enforcement problems that this would create, it would remove parental freedom to leave things to their children. If both values are regarded as important, then the policy outcome is likely to involve a compromise between the two, such as an inheritance tax with allowances and exemptions and a marginal rate much less than 100 per cent.

More generally, it is likely that any actual policy prescription is likely to involve trading off one value against another, as discussed in Chapter 3. In consequence, full equality of choices will never be achieved. However, that does not mean that equality of choices is not a worthwhile aim for which to strive, any more than the fact that individual liberties have on occasion to be circumscribed in the interests of preserving some other values implies that freedom is not a worthwhile social objective. A society with less inequality in choice sets will be one with less inequity; the challenge for policy is to move in the direction of greater equality of choices, and hence greater equity, without too serious a compromise of other values.

Notes: Chapter 6

1   An earlier version of this argument appears in Le Grand (1984a).
    Economists who have discussed equality of choice sets include
    Musgrave (1976), Gordon (1976), Archibald and Donaldson (1979)
    and Sen (1980, 1985). Musgrave, Gordon, and Archibald and
    Donaldson discussed choice sets defined over commodities; Sen defines
    choice sets over 'functionings' (roughly, the range of things that an
    individual can do with the commodities under her command, given
    her personal characteristics); these he terms capability sets. Political
    philosophers and others have also paid attention to the related concep-
    tion of equality of resources, particularly in recent years; see, for
    example, Dworkin (1981a, 1981b), Roemer (1986), Abell (1989),
    Arneson (1989) and Cohen (1989). Some of these contributions are
    discussed in the main text; but at this point it is important to note
    that, with the exception of Arneson and Cohen, none of these dis-
    cussed the relationship between equality of resources and the extent of
    individual control.
        Another distributional principle that may be consistent with the
    concept of equity as choice is the argument by Goodin (1985) for 'pro-
    tecting the vulnerable', where he proposes that those who are vulner-
    able to our actions and choices have a claim on us. Although he is not
    putting forward this idea explicitly as a principle of equity or justice,
    it could be regarded as consistent with equity as choice because, almost
    by definition, our actions and choices are beyond the control of those
    vulnerable to them.
2   See, for example, Dworkin (1981a, 1981b) and Cohen (1989).
    Dworkin argues that justice requires equality of endowments (which he
    terms resources) and not, for example, equality of welfare. Preferences
    are irrelevant. Cohen agrees that inequalities in endowments are
    inequitable, but argues that there may be occasions when differences
    in preferences can also cause inequity. This is discussed further in the
    main text.
3   Cohen puts forward this point in his criticism of Dworkin's position
    that justice only requires equality of resources. But it also applies to,
    for example, Sen's equality of capabilities. The relevant 'cut', in
    Cohen's phrase, is not between either resources or capabilities on the
    one hand and preferences on the other, but between factors within and
    outside individual control.
4   The idea is discussed in (and probably originates with) Goodin (1988,
    pp. 291–6). Goodin actually raises it in the context of a discussion of
    general principles of desert, with no specific reference to equity as
    choice; however, it is clearly applicable to the latter.

7 Equity, health and health care

Late at night, a car being driven at speed mounts the pavement and and hits a pedestrian out walking her dog. The car then crashes into a wall. Both the driver and the pedestrian are critically injured and are taken to the nearest hospital, where it is discovered that the pedestrian was sober but that the driver has concentrations of alcohol in his blood that are well above the legal limit. There is only one emergency bed available in the hospital. Moreover, the hospital is a private one; the driver has medical insurance, but the pedestrian has none.

In this situation, who should receive priority of treatment? Should it be the pedestrian, on the grounds that she was not at fault? Or should it be the driver, who has the means to pay for the treatment? If it is the pedestrian, then who should meet the costs of her treatment? Should she meet her own costs through a direct payment? Should her costs be met by the driver, as the one responsible for her accident? Or should the costs be met by the wider community in some way?

The issues raised by this example are part of a wider set of questions concerning the allocation of health care and the distribution of its costs. Given that health care is a scarce commodity, how should it be allocated between individuals? How should the costs of health care be distributed? Should they be met by the individuals who directly benefit from it?

Or should they be met by the state, on behalf of the community as a whole? To what extent, if any, should people be responsible for the medical care of others? Should health care be privately or publicly financed and provided?

Health economists and others have given these questions a good deal of attention in recent years. However, most of the work has concentrated on the *efficiency* of alternative arrangements for the finance and delivery of health care; much less attention has been paid to the *equity* of those arrangements.[1] This is unfortunate, because equity is in the forefront of public interest in the allocation of health care. The importance of attaining equity aims, such as 'equal treatment for equal need', 'equality of access to health care' and similar ends are invariably emphasized in debates on the issue, frequently dominating all other considerations.[2]

Not only are systematic discussions of the issue rare, but such as there are rarely attempt properly to define conceptions of equity in this context, or to locate such conceptions, in a wider philosophical framework. What are the grounds for considering, for instance, equal treatment for equal need or equality of access to health care as reasonable interpretations of equity? Are there occasions where inequity would persist even if either or both of these kinds of equality were achieved? If so, and we shall see that there are indeed occasions when this might be so, is there any other basis on which we can construct an interpretation of equity that could serve as a guide to health policy? It is to these questions that this chapter is addressed.

The chapter begins with an examination of the concepts of equal treatment for equal need and equality of access, as those perhaps the most prominent in the debate concerning equity and health care.[3] This leads to a consideration of the underlying question concerning the equity of the distribution of health itself. A final section considers some of the implications of the discussion for policy.

Equal treatment for equal need

The idea that each individual with the same 'need' for health care should receive the same treatment is of considerable intuitive appeal. This in large part derives from its principal implication: that the distribution of medical care should be independent of the distribution of income, wealth or any other form of economic or political power. For it does seem unjust if, of two individuals with the same diagnosed illness, one receives better treatment than the other simply because she is wealthier, better educated, or has more influential connections.

There are obvious problems with the interpretation of this concept in practice, notably with the interpretation of need. But this is not the issue I want to address here.[4] I shall simply define need in terms of ill-health and ask the question whether it is always the case that equal treatment for equal need (equal 'amounts' of ill-health) is equitable and unequal treatment for equal need inequitable.

Consider the example of the drunken driver and the pedestrian with which this chapter opened. On the assumption that both are equally injured, who should get the emergency bed? Since it is impossible to treat both, the only way of achieving 'equal' treatment for equal need is for neither to get treated: a ludicrous outcome. A less strict interpretation of the principle might require allocating the bed on the toss of a coin: each then has an equal *probability* of obtaining treatment. Yet this seems rather arbitrary: would we really be content if the coin landed in such a way that the drunken driver was treated while the pedestrian died from her injuries? I think most people would find it more acceptable to allocate the bed to the pedestrian, on the grounds that the driver was, to a large extent, at fault for his predicament, whereas she was not.

Or consider the similar example used by Glover (1977,

p. 225). Suppose there is one place in the intensive care unit, and two people in need of it are brought into the hospital. One is a seriously wounded bank robber and the other is a man who was equally seriously wounded when he heroically went to the aid of a policeman under fire from the bank robber. Who should get the place in the intensive care unit? Most people, Glover thinks, would opt for giving the place to the 'hero'; he in some sense deserves the place by virtue of his actions, while the bank robber has disqualified himself for the same reasons.

But what of situations where resources are less scarce? Should the only consideration determining the allocation of medical care be need? Some would say yes: for Bernard Williams (1962), 'the proper ground for the distribution of medical care is ill-health' (p. 121). Goodin (1988) also argues that 'needs trump deserts', although he does allow for the use of desert considerations to break a tie, as in the single emergency bed example (pp. 296–8). However, it is not clear why, if deserts have a role in breaking ties, they do not have a role in determining the allocation of resources in other situations. The single emergency bed is simply an extreme example of scarce resources; in practice, resources are always scarce to some degree, and priorities will have to be established. 'Need' will undoubtedly be an important criterion in determining priorities, but it is far from clear that it should always be the dominating criterion.

Moreover, even if need were accepted as the dominating criterion, it would not necessarily be identical with equity. If the drunken driver were slightly more seriously injured than the pedestrian, then the need criterion would require his receiving priority of treatment. Although this might be acceptable on grounds other than equity (compassion, for instance), it is not obvious that it would automatically be *equitable* or fair.

Another problem with the conception can be illustrated

by an example of two individuals equally ill, each with the same capacity to respond to medical treatment. Suppose they are also identical in all other respects, *except* in their attitudes towards risk: in situations involving uncertainty, one is much more cautious than the other. Now each is offered the opportunity of an operation: an operation that offers a good chance of complete recovery but also has a measurable probability of leaving permanent physical damage. In this situation, the more risk-averse individual may choose not to have the operation, whereas the other may choose to go ahead. In that case, there would not be equal treatment for equal need; but it is unlikely that many would regard that outcome as inequitable. The fact that the risk-averse individual had *chosen* not to have the operation is critical; the difference in treatment arises from choice and hence does not seem prima facie inequitable.

A way out of the difficulty posed by this example is to argue that the focus for equity purposes should be upon equality of opportunity or access, rather than on equality of treatment. Individuals should have the same opportunity of treatment; whether they choose to avail themselves of that opportunity is up to them. However, this too presents difficulties.

Equality of access

Equality of access and equal treatment for equal need are often confused. But as has been pointed out by several authors (see, for example, Mooney 1986, and Olsen and Rogers, forthcoming), access to treatment is purely a supply-side phenomenon, whereas the amount of treatment actually received depends on the interaction of both supply and demand. So, as in the example of the two individuals with different attitudes towards risk, people may have equal access to treatment; some may choose to accept the treatment on offer, but some may not. In such a case there would be equality of access, but not equality of treatment.

Equality of access can be defined in a variety of ways. One is that all individuals should face the same prices (monetary and non-monetary) for medical treatment (Le Grand 1982, p. 15; Mooney 1986, p. 108). If some individuals are charged more than others, or they have to travel further, or they are required to wait longer for medical treatment, then they face a higher personal cost of treatment than others and hence there is inequality of access.

However, equality of access in this sense may well conflict with intuitive conceptions of equity. To take just one example, suppose some wealthy individuals choose to buy a country house in a remote rural region. Do they have the right to expect the same access to top quality medical facilities as anyone else? Should expensive facilities be built in the region in order to bring their personal travel costs down to, say, those faced by the residents of an inner-city area close to a teaching hospital? Or should helicopters be laid on for their special use at no charge?

To answer no to these questions is not to imply that *all* people who live in remote areas should not have equality of access to health care facilities. Poor families, or those who for some other reason are 'locked into' a location that is poorly endowed with facilities, could well be viewed as suffering inequitable differences in access. But there does not seem to be so strong an argument for equality of access for people who have freely chosen to live in those areas. More generally, where people have a degree of choice about their situation and therefore about their access to medical or other facilities, any resultant inequalities in access do not seem to be necessarily inequitable.

But, as has been pointed out by Olsen and Rogers (forthcoming), there is a more fundamental problem with the definition of equal access in terms of equal prices. Most people might agree that if, for reasons beyond their control, people with the *same* incomes faced unequal prices then there is indeed inequality of access. But the idea that equal access would be obtained if people with *different* incomes faced the same set of prices might be less acceptable. A poor individual paying the same price as a rich individual will be making a larger 'sacrifice' in some sense and therefore will not have the same access to the commodity concerned.

Olsen and Rogers' preferred definition is one where individuals are considered to have equal access to a good if and only if they are able to consume the same quantity of that good. The distinction is summarized in Figure 7.1. Suppose there are two individuals and two commodities, 1 and 2, one of which is health care (commodity 1). The quantities consumed of each commodity are denoted by x_1 and x_2 and are

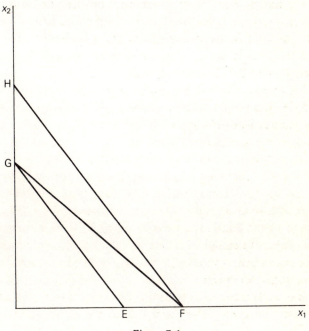

Figure 7.1

plotted along the horizontal and vertical axes respectively. One individual is richer than the other and has a budget line, HF, that lies outside the other's budget line, GE. However, the two lines are parallel, indicating that the ratio of the prices faced by the two individuals are the same, and therefore that equality of access (to both commodities) in the first sense has been achieved. However, it has not been achieved in the Olsen and Rogers sense, for the poorer individual cannot consume the same quantities of x_1 as the richer one. Equality of access in that sense would be achieved if the price of health care to the poorer individual was reduced, shifting her budget line to GF – in which case, it should be noted, equality of access in the first sense would now be violated.

For the reasons already given, it is probable that people with a concern for equity in the allocation of health care would not find the first interpretation of equality of access fully acceptable. However, it is not clear that they would find the Olsen and Rogers interpretation acceptable either. For, as Olsen and Rogers themselves acknowledge, if the two individuals choose the same quantity of medical care, they will not have the same quantity of other commodities. The poorer individual is still having to make a larger sacrifice than the richer one, in that she can only have the same standard of medical treatment by having a lower standard of living in other respects.

However, as Olsen and Rogers point out, the only way that this objection can be overcome is for every one to have the same choice sets defined over the relevant commodities. And this seems to imply that the conception of equity implicit in the idea of equality of access to medical care is simply that of full equality of overall choices. But this is not wholly satisfactory either, for, as Olsen and Rogers argue, it does not seem to capture the concern for access to a particular good.

It is in fact the emphasis on a particular good that is

striking about the ideas both of equal treatment for equal need and equality of access. The idea that some goods are special in terms of the criteria to be applied to their distribution has received attention from both economists and political philosophers. Musgrave (1959) termed such goods 'merit' goods; Tobin (1970) has called the idea 'specific egalitarianism'; it is discussed by Weale (1983) and underlies Walzer's notion of 'spheres of justice' where he argues that different criteria of justice apply in different areas of economic and social life (Walzer 1983).

But simply to point to the fact that some goods seem to be of particular concern for equity purposes begs the question of why this should be so. In particular, why is equity in the distribution of medical care (or in access to medical care) singled out as being of more concern than, say, the distribution of televisions? Many writers have addressed this issue, including Nozick (1974), Weale (1983), Daniels (1985) and Klein (1988). However, none of these referred to what seems to be the most plausible reason for this particularity of concern. This derives from most peoples' perspective of the cause of the demand for health care: a cause, ill-health, that is viewed as being beyond individual control. On this view, people do not choose to become ill; hence, their demand for treatment if they do become ill is of a qualitatively different nature than their demand for televisions. The fact that most people would use the term 'need' rather than demand in the context of medical care reinforces the point; for, as noted in the previous chapter, the concept of need suggests something beyond individual control.

Whether the view that the 'need' for health care is beyond individual control is correct or not, what this argument suggests is that questions concerning the equity of the distribution of health care cannot be separated from those concerning the equity of the underlying distribution of health itself. And this needs some more extensive discussion.

Equality of health

Although, as noted above, there has been relatively little discussion of the meaning of equity in the context of health
care, there has been even less of the meaning of the equitable distribution of health. What is a fair or just distribution of health? Should the aim of an equitable health
policy be to equalize everyone's health states, so far as that
might be possible? Should the aim be to promote equal
access to health? Or are there reasons why, on the grounds
of social justice or equity, some people 'ought' to have better
health than others?

The failure to address these questions is in some ways
rather curious. To focus on the equitable distribution of
health care rather than on that of health itself seems to be
putting the cart before the horse. Presumably, the concern
for the equity or otherwise of a particular distribution of
health care must have its roots in a more basic concern for
the health of the individual in receipt of such care. If that
is the case, then the equitable distribution of health care can
only really be equitable if it contributes to an equitable
distribution of health. Establishing the meaning of the latter
ought therefore logically to be prior to establishing the
meaning of the former.

One possible justification for concentrating on equity in
the context of health care rather than in the context of health
is because health care can be distributed or redistributed by
acts of policy in a way that health itself cannot. Since individuals' health is located within themselves it is impossible
to take away someone's health and give it to another; that
is, it is impossible to 'redistribute' health. On the other
hand, it is possible to redistribute health care facilities
between individuals. Hence, it could be argued, health care
is amenable to policies concerned with promoting equity in
a way that health is not. Therefore, it makes more sense to

talk of the equity or otherwise of the distribution of health care than of the distribution of health.

But this is not very compelling. Although in one sense it is true that it is impossible to redistribute health, this does not mean that the distribution of health is insensitive to public policy. For it is obviously possible to influence by policy many of the factors that *affect* health, such as nutrition, housing and work conditions, and, of course, medical care itself. Moreover, the factors that affect the consequences of ill-health are also amenable to policy: the distribution of spectacles, or of aids to the disabled, for example. Hence, any evaluation of the relevant policies must involve an evaluation of their health outcomes; and, if part of that evaluation concerns equity, then it is essential to have a conception of what constitutes an equitable health outcome.

Perhaps a more convincing explanation of the absence of discussion concerning the meaning of equity in the context of health is that it is automatically presumed that here at least inequality means inequity. For instance, in the extensive literature on the extent and causes of inequalities in health there seems to be an unquestioned assumption that such inequalities are automatically unacceptable (see, for example, Black 1980, p. 3).

But, again, consideration of some simple cases suggests that the link is by no means automatic. In the example with which the chapter opened, does the drunken driver, who knocks over an innocent pedestrian but who is also injured himself in the accident, have an equal claim to full restoration to health as his victim? Do heavy smokers who contract lung cancer have the same claim, on equity grounds, to resources to restore them to full health (so far as that might be possible) as non-smokers who contract the disease? Are drivers who refuse to put on seat-belts, or motor-cyclists who refuse to wear helmets, entitled to as much compensation in the event of an accident as those who do take those precautions? More generally, should not those who consciously and voluntarily assume health risks in order to undertake some activity solely of benefit to themselves bear the consequences if these prove adverse?

Choice and health

What the above suggests is that the history of a particular distribution of health is crucial to any decision concerning its equity. And the crucial factor concerning that history is the extent to which it arose through individuals' choices. If an individual's ill-health results from factors beyond his or her control, then the situation is inequitable; if it results from factors within his or her control, then it is equitable.

The point can be illustrated as follows. Suppose a particular activity is known to have an adverse effect on health, especially if undertaken to excess. An obvious example would be smoking; others include heavy drinking, driving too fast, and working in a hazardous or stressful environment. Then there is a trade-off between health and the activity concerned.

This is illustrated in Figure 7.2. In that diagram an individual's state of health, h, (assumed to be measurable) is plotted along the vertical axis, and the quantity of the health-harming activity, q, along the horizontal axis. The curve RST is a health frontier: the horizontal section RS of the frontier reflects an assumption that indulgence in the activity only begins adversely to affect health after a certain level; the concave section ST reflects the assumption that after that level it does so at an ever-increasing rate.

In practice, the exact position and shape of this frontier will differ between individuals, depending on their physique, nutrition, etc. But let us consider two individuals, A and B, for whom the frontier is identical. Assume that both derive pleasure from the health-harming activity. In fact, if

they did not know of its adverse health consequences and
their only constraints were the price of the activity (relative
to other prices) and their incomes, each would have
demanded a level of the activity greater than OT; but
actually they both are fully aware of the effects on health
and, therefore, moderate their levels of the activity. Assume,
too, that both derive satisfaction from good health, either
directly or through its enabling them to obtain greater
pleasure from other activities. However, suppose that individual A derives more pleasure at the margin from the
activity, relative to that derived from health, than individual
B. These assumptions are incorporated in the indifference
curves U_a (for individual A) and U_b (for B) in Figure 7.2.

It is apparent from Figure 7.2 that individual A's equilibrium level of the activity (determined by the point at
which U_a is tangent to RST) is greater than individual B's
(where U_b is tangent to RST); and that, as a result, his health

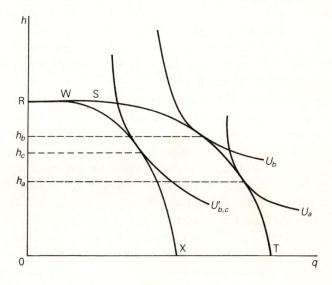

Figure 7.2

(h_a) is worse than her's (h_b). But this does not seem inequitable. Both were fully aware of the dangers involved; both were unconstrained in their choice by other factors; both have made informed decisions based on their own preferences. The results of those decisions are different, and that is reflected in disparities in their health states; but that is the outcome of their own decision, exercised over the same range of choices, and hence is not inequitable.

Now consider a third individual, C. This person has the same preferences (the same indifference map) as B, but a rather different health-frontier. In particular, she is poorer than B, has a lower level of nutrition and is less able to withstand the ravages of the health-harming activity. Her frontier therefore takes the shape RWX; her equilibrium health level is h_c, below that of individual B.

Now in this case the difference between the health states of individuals B and C does seem inequitable. It has arisen not because of any differences in preferences between the two individuals; if B had faced the same health possibility frontier as C, she would have made the same choices, and had the same level of health. Rather it has arisen because the individuals do not face the same health frontier; for reasons beyond their control they do not face the same choices over health and health-related activities.

This notion can be expressed more formally by adopting the definition of the previous chapter that a distribution is equitable if it is the outcome of individuals making choices under equal constraints. That is, disparities in health states that arise from fully-informed individuals exercising autonomous preferences facing the same range of choices over health and health-related activities are not inequitable; but disparities in health that can be directly related to differences in the constraints facing those individuals are inequitable.

Again, the chief merit of this interpretation concerns its ability to capture the essence of the term equity, at least as used in this context. Most of the examples used above to challenge the other conceptions of equity involved the presence or absence of choice. Thus the drunken driver, the individual refusing the risky operation, or the wealthy people who preferred to live in a rural area all had a degree of choice in their situation, which thereby did not automatically qualify as inequitable. On the other hand, those who, through factors beyond their control, responded slowly to medical treatment seemed to have a good claim on equity grounds for more of the treatment than those who responded more quickly.

However, its application in practice does raise a number of problems. One concerns the question of 'autonomous' preferences and the status of the choices that result when those preferences are exercised. Ever since Grossman's pioneering work on the demand for health (1972), health economists have accepted that health states can be modelled as the outcome of individuals exercising choices within constraints. But to social scientists and others less imbued with the notion of economic man or woman such notions often appear preposterous. They might argue that no preferences are fully (or even partly) autonomous; they are simply the product of social and biological forces and thus are as much beyond individuals' control as the constraints they face. Hence, autonomous choice does not exist; all disparities in health (or indeed in any other behavioural outcome, including health care) are therefore inequitable.

If this view is fully accepted, then indeed all health differences are unjust or unfair; and inequality in health is synonymous with inequity in health. However, as was argued in Chapter 6, to accept it fully involves a complete denial of free will: a momentous step with implications that stretch well beyond the concerns of health policy. Most health specialists would now agree that individuals have some degree of control over their health – although they would doubtless differ on the *extent* of that control. The question for policy purposes then becomes one of ascertaining the degree to which a particular health outcome is the result of the constraints faced by an individual and to what extent the result of his or her preferences. We turn to this in the broader questions of the implications of the discussion for policy of the next section.

Before doing so, however, it is necessary to clear up one misconception concerning the idea of equity as choice. Pereira (1989) has criticized the argument on the grounds that, in the examples used, the choice sets concerned are defined over 'fundamental commodities' (such as health and smoking); rather, he argues, it is preferable to consider equality in 'basic capabilities' as advocated by Sen. However, the critical insight of the analysis here does not concern the items over which the choice set is defined; it concerns the extent of choice involved in each case. As Cohen (1989) has pointed out, the relevant distinction is not between commodities and capabilities, but between factors that are within individual control and those that are beyond it. Hence, if there are differences between individuals' 'basic capabilities' due to factors within their control, then any health differences that ensue are not inequitable.

Implications for policy

Suppose it were accepted that some conception such as this did form a reasonable basis for determining an equitable distribution of health. What would be the implications for policy towards the distribution and the finance of health care?

The simplest cases are those where it is clear that individuals have illnesses that are entirely due to factors beyond their control. Examples are illnesses that are 'inherited', either through a genetic deficiency of some kind or through family circumstances during childhood (diseases that are the consequence of malnutrition due to family poverty, for instance). Since they have a pre-existing condition, such individuals are unlikely to be able to obtain private health insurance, even if they wished to do so. In such cases it seems equitable that such individuals be offered health care that is free at the point of use and that is financed by the community as a whole.

A similar situation arises when individuals become ill through lack of knowledge concerning a particular health risk: for example, food poisoning that results from eating something accidentally contaminated by industrial pollution. Again, it seems clear that individuals in this situation are ill for reasons beyond their control and, therefore, should be offered treatment free at the point of use. It may also seem clear who should pay for the treatment: the person or persons responsible for creating the health risk, on the assumption that they can be identified. However, this is not quite so simple, for reasons to be discussed in a moment.

The pedestrian/drunken driver example with which the chapter opened falls into this category. The pedestrian went out to walk her dog without knowing that there was any danger from the drunken driver and, therefore, that she was incurring a health risk by so doing; hence, she has been injured through no fault of her own, and she should be offered free treatment. Again, it might seem obvious that the person who should pay for her treatment is the driver; but again this is not so simple, as we shall see.

What of situations where individuals voluntarily incur health risks in the full knowledge of what they are doing? Examples here are the motor cyclist who rides without his helmet; the motorist who drives without a seat-belt; the smoker who knows of the health risks associated with her habit but nonetheless continues smoking. It might seem, at first, that they have forfeited any claim on the community's resources; they have made a voluntary choice, in full awareness of the risks involved, and they should therefore bear the full costs of any health consequences that might ensue. As

Weale (1978) argues, 'a just distribution of health resources need not compensate for the increased health risks that people voluntarily incur' (p. 74). This argument presumably implies that either these people should not receive treatment if there is not enough available after those whose claims are more legitimate have been met (as in the bank robber case), or that they should pay the full costs of any treatment they might receive.

However, this does not seem quite correct. Take the example of the smoker, and suppose that there is a one-in-five chance of developing cancer through smoking. In this situation, not every smoker will develop cancer; indeed, 80 per cent will not. The 20 per cent who do are the victims not solely of their own choices, but, at least in one sense, of bad luck. Hence, their health in such a situation is in large part an outcome of a random 'lottery' and thus beyond their control – except in so far as they chose to enter the lottery. Similarly with the drunken driver example: he did not actually choose to become seriously injured and the fact that he did is in part due to bad luck.

In such cases, as was argued in Chapter 6, the solution lies in a calculation of the expected value of the losses involved.[5] So, if there is a 20 per cent probability of contracting a particular disease from an activity, then each person undertaking the activity is responsible for one-fifth of the costs of contracting it, *whether or not* they actually acquire it. In practice, this outcome could be achieved by compelling any individual undertaking the activity concerned to take out an appropriate amount of insurance. Alternatively, a charge could be levied on the activity itself (for example, a tax on cigarettes), the revenue from which would be used to pay for the treatment and caring costs of those who acquired the disease from undertaking the activity.

However, the problems for the conception posed by the existence of risk are broader than this. Almost every situation in which normal healthy individuals find themselves involves some risk to their health: driving, accidents in the home, contracting infections through contacts with others, and so forth. In that case, almost every case of ill-health can be partly laid at the door of the constraints that individuals face, and partly at the door of their autonomous preferences. How, then, should costs of treatment be allocated?

Again, this difficulty can be resolved by mobilizing the idea of expected value. We can illustrate the arguments by use of a more formal example. Suppose each individual in society faces an equal probability, p, in each year of contracting a disease with treatment costs, L. Suppose, further, that there is no practical way of avoiding this risk and that the treatment costs are the only costs (either private or social) associated with the disease. Then equity would be achieved if each individual were charged an annual amount equal to the expected value of the loss, pL, and if all treatment were provided free at the point of use. The revenue raised through the charge would be used to meet the treatment cost for those unfortunate enough to contract the disease; if the correct estimates of p and L were used, then this revenue would be exactly sufficient to meet this cost.

As economists will recognize, the amount pL is the premium that would be charged in a perfectly competitive insurance market, with perfect information, no transaction costs and no moral hazard. Such a market would also be Pareto-efficient. Therefore, it might appear at first sight that the optimal policy in this situation would be to encourage such a market, thus achieving equity and efficiency simultaneously.

However, such an inference would be premature. There would be two groups uninsured in such a market: those who would have purchased health insurance if they had not had choice sets that were too small (the 'poor'), and those who had reasonably sized choice sets but who preferred to accept the risk of loss rather than pay the necessary insurance premium. Now the exclusion of the first group clearly arises from their constraints; hence, any losses they incur through the absence of insurance would be inequitable. However, in an ideal world, it is not clear that the appropriate policy response to their situation would be through the system for the delivery and finance of health care. The problems faced by those with small choice sets with respect to the consumption of health care are the same as the problems they face with respect to their consumption of any good or service; they have fewer choices overall than others, and hence the decision to purchase any commodity will involve them in a greater sacrifice. The appropriate way of achieving greater equity, therefore, is to reduce the difference between their overall choice sets and those of the rest of society.

This reduction can be achieved in a variety of ways, including the redistribution of income or the lowering of some or all of the prices they face. The lowering of the price of a commodity will bias the choices they make towards the purchasing of that commodity; and, if that commodity is socially acceptable, as arguably health care is, it may be politically easier to increase the size of the choice set faced by the poor by lowering the price of that commodity than by redistributing income. If this is the case for health care, then the appropriate policy response is to subsidize the price of health insurance for the poor.

Those in the second group – the non-risk averse – are also problematic. Because of the structure of their preferences they have chosen not to be insured. Hence, it could be argued that any individual contracting the disease incurs losses that are in some sense voluntary, and therefore she has no equity claim.

However, as with the smoking example, this does not seem to be quite correct. Such individuals have not chosen to bear the full cost of contracting the disease; rather, they have chosen to incur the risk of bearing that loss. If they do in fact contract the disease, since in part their subsequent losses would be due to bad luck, it would not necessarily be equitable for them to bear the full cost, L. It would be preferable, on equity grounds, for them to be brought into the same system as everyone else: that is, paying pL whether or not they contracted the disease and receiving any required treatment free.

Thus, it seems as though we cannot rely on a perfectly competitive insurance market to be equitable. A more equitable alternative would be for a government agency to offer health care free at the point of use and to finance it through a compulsory charge or tax on all individuals, regardless of their attitude to risk. The revenues from the tax should go to finance health care; that is, the tax should be hypothecated. If the underlying distribution of overall choice sets was inequitable, then the tax should be progressive, thus contributing to an overall equalization of choice sets. In addition, if it were established that some activities (such as smoking) did create greater health risks than others, then a special extra tax should be levied on those activities, at a level sufficient to generate enough revenue to finance the extra treatment costs. Again the special tax would be hypothecated.

Finally, we should return to the question flagged above of whether those such as drunken drivers, who create a health risk for others, should be liable for any costs that thereby ensue. Again, it is not clear that they should be liable for all those costs, since in part the costs will arise from bad luck. On the other hand, it is also not clear that those who create a health risk, but who through good luck do not actually cause any ill-health, should be liable for nothing. Again, it would be preferable that those who create a health risk for others by undertaking certain activities should be treated in the same way as those who create a health risk for themselves: they should pay a hypothecated tax on the activity concerned, the revenues from which should pay for the costs of any treatment that may be necessary, either for themselves or for anyone else affected.

Obviously, these ideas need further development. In particular, the model on which they are constructed is far from the real world. In that world, there are different diseases, each with different treatment costs and different risks of contracting them; not all losses are insurable or can be adequately compensated by cash payments; information is imperfect, as are the institutions that try to use the information. To include such complications and, more generally, to assess the implications of applying this conception of equity in the detailed formulation of policy towards all aspects of health and health care is a task beyond the scope of this chapter. But it is hoped that enough has been said to indicate the lines along which such an endeavour might proceed.

Conclusion

It may seem surprising that, despite starting from an 'individualistic' notion of equity, we have emerged with the policy recommendation of a 'collectivist' health care system that is free at the point of use and mostly financed from a progressive tax. Indeed, an earlier version of this argument (Le Grand 1987) was criticized for importing further value judgements in order to obtain this conclusion (Pereira 1989). It is therefore worth recapitulating the stages of the reasoning that led to this outcome to see whether such importing is actually going on.

The reasoning begins with the proposition derived from the arguments of earlier chapters that differences in the health status of individuals that arise from choice are equitable, whereas those that derive from factors beyond individual control are not. It follows from this that people who are struck by ill-health because of factors that are clearly beyond their control, such as their genetic inheritance, their family background, or because, through no fault of their own, they were poorly informed, should not suffer losses in consequence; hence, they should have treatment free at the point of use and financed by the community. But even people who voluntarily assume a risk of loss due to ill-health are not responsible for *all* the losses they incur if the risk goes against them, for they too are in part the victim of bad luck, a factor beyond their control; rather, they are responsible for the 'expected value' of those losses. Hence, in cases where the risk is clearly identified with certain activities (such as smoking), everyone who undertakes the activities concerned should bear these costs, whether or not the outcome is adverse to their health; an obvious mechanism for achieving this is to tax the activity concerned and to use the revenues to finance the treatment for those for whom the outcome is adverse. In cases where health risks are not obviously identifiable, then everyone is in some sense at equal risk and, therefore, everyone should bear the expected value of the relevant losses. Hence, there should be a uniform tax to finance all other health care.

An exception to this arises if it is considered easier to reduce overall inequality in the constraints that people face by reducing the price of health care rather than by other methods of resource redistribution. In that case the tax should be graduated by income.

From this it should be apparent that further value judgements have not been imported into the analysis. Some *empirical* judgements have indeed been made, particularly about the presence of risk; indeed, it is the existence of risk that is the driving force behind the collectivist solution. But judgements of fact are not the same as judgements of value and should not be confused with them. Moreover, an assessment of the realities of the situation are an inevitable part of policy recommendations, which have to take account of the world as it is.

Notes: Chapter 7

1   The contributions of health economists to the question of the efficiency of alternative systems of health care finance and delivery are legion.

The principal arguments are summarized in Le Grand, Propper and Robinson (1991, ch. 2), Maynard and Williams (1984), Mooney (1986) and Barr (1987).

The literature on the equity of these arrangements, although small, is increasing. However, most of the contributions have been concerned, not with normative questions on how health care should be distributed, as here, but with empirical questions concerning the actual distribution of health and health care. Writers who have dealt explicitly with normative issues concerning equity and health care include Mooney (1986), Daniels (1985), the contributors to Green (1988) and Pereira (1989). The last of these provides a useful review of the literature. An earlier version of some of the arguments in this chapter appeared in Le Grand (1987).

2 This has been acknowledged by leading health economists. For example, Reinhardt has observed that there are currently three desiderata that universally dominate health goals: equity, the freedom of health care providers' practice, and budgetary and economic control. Quoting him with approval, McLachlan and Maynard (1982) add 'the vast majority of the population would elect for equity to be the prime consideration' (p. 556), a view endorsed by Mooney (1986, p. 145).

3 They do not of course exhaust all possible interpretations of equity in the health care context. Others are considered by Le Grand (1987) and Pereira (1989). Most of these are applications of more general rules such as envy-free allocations, utilitarianism, the Rawls maximin principle and the Sen capabilities approach. The arguments concerning the unsuitability of these kind of approaches for interpreting equity in the health care context are simply part of the wider arguments concerning their unsuitability for interpreting equity in general; these were discussed in earlier chapters and need not be repeated here.

An exception that does concern health specifically is 'health maximization', advocated by Culyer (1988), and discussed extensively by Pereira (1989). Under this rule a distribution of health care would be considered desirable if it served to maximize the sum of individuals' health (as measured by, for instance, the number of quality-adjusted life-years or QALYs they had open to them). As pointed out by Pereira, the principal difficulty with this approach is the same as that with other maximization rules, such as utilitarianism: that it is primarily concerned with aggregates rather than with distributions (see above, p. 92).

4 This issue has been extensively discussed elsewhere; for perhaps the most lucid treatment, see A. Williams (1978). For a broader discussion of the meaning of need, and one that takes a rather different line from that offered here, see Doyal and Gough (1984).

5 For a similar argument, see Goodin (1988, p. 294).

8 Equity and grants to local governments

In most countries with political subdivisions, grants from central to local governments are an important part of the fiscal scene. In the United Kingdom, about half of all local government spending is financed through grants from the central government. In the United States, about 30 per cent of state and 45 per cent of local revenues come from higher level governments. In Australia the equivalent figures are 60 per cent for state and 25 per cent for local; in West Germany they are 20 per cent for the *Lander* and 45 per cent for local government. [1]

The scale of these grants means that the criteria upon which they are distributed are of considerable importance; and for most of the countries concerned, equity considerations play a crucial role in determining those criteria. [2] Hence, this seems an appropriate area in which to provide another illustration of how the more philosophical discussion of earlier chapters can be applied to a specific policy problem.

The main argument is presented in the first section of this chapter. Under some restrictive assumptions, conclusions are derived concerning the principal sources of inequity between local governments, and a scheme is proposed for eliminating them. In the next section, the assumptions are relaxed, and the scheme modified accordingly. Difficulties in defining and measuring some of the concepts involved are discussed in the

following section. The conclusions are summarized at the
end of the chapter. The discussion requires some familiarity
with the algebra of tax and grant formulae, but otherwise
should not present too much difficulty to non-specialists.

Sources of inequity

The arguments of earlier chapters imply that fiscal disparities
between local governments should be considered inequitable
if they arise from factors that are largely or entirely beyond
the control of the relevant agents. If, for instance, one local
government has to levy a higher tax rate than another to
provide the same public services, because it has a lower tax
base and/or higher costs per unit of public services, then this
would be judged inequitable – as long as its tax base and/or
cost structure are regarded as beyond its control. If, on the
other hand, a government is levying a higher tax rate than
another simply because it wishes to provide a higher level of
public services, then this can be viewed as a matter of local
preferences and, as long as these are regarded as being
within local control, the disparity would not be inequitable.
Differences that arise from autonomous preferences do not
constitute inequity; disparities that arise from unavoidable
circumstances do.

In order to develop these propositions and to draw out
their implications for the development of a system of grants
for local governments, it is useful to conduct the initial
discussion under the following simple assumptions.
Subsequently they will be relaxed.

(a) Each local government spends an annual sum per head
     of its population, L_i, on providing one public service at
     a level per head of B_i and at a cost per unit of P_i. Thus:

$$L_i = P_i B_i$$

(b) Each government has one principal source of revenue: a tax levied at an annual rate, E_i, on a per capita base of Y_i. If the per capita value of revenue raised is denoted by T_i, then the total revenue per head is:

$$T_i = E_i Y_i$$

(c) No government can influence its costs per unit provision of public services or its tax base per head. P_i and Y_i are fixed.

(d) Each government's public services are for the benefit only of its residents, who benefit equally; and its taxes are paid only by its residents.

(e) A government's total revenue per head in any one year equals the sum of its expenditure on public services and any savings it may undertake. Those savings could be negative (i.e. it dis-saves from past accumulated funds or borrows). If the net savings position of a local government per head of its population is denoted by A_i (for accumulation), then this assumption requires:

$$T_i = L_i + A_i$$

$A_i >$, $<$ or $= 0$ as the government saves, dis-saves or borrows, or balances its budget.

(f) Each government has complete discretion over the amount of public services per head that it provides (B_i).

(g) There is no migration from one local government area to another.

In these circumstances, local governments may differ in their levels of public service per head (B_i), their taxation and expenditure per head (T_i, L_i), their tax rate (E_i), their rateable value per head (Y_i), their costs per unit (P_i) and their net savings per head (A_i). We must consider which of these differences is inequitable.

By assumption (f), local governments are free to vary their public services without restriction. Hence, differences in these can arise from local preferences and, therefore, are not necessarily inequitable according to our definition. This is not a surprising conclusion: it is doubtful whether anyone today would consider total equalization of local public services an appropriate objective for an intergovernmental grants scheme designed to promote equity, although it does seem to have been implicit in much of the earlier treatments of the subject (see, for example, Webb 1920, pp. 16–17). A similar objection applies to the equalization of the absolute levels of taxation or expenditure per head.

A more interesting suggestion is that of Thurow (1970). He argued that it is not differences in the level of public services per head that should be considered, but differences in the ratio of the levels to the amount of tax 'effort', as measured by the tax rate. Disparities in this ratio, which he terms the benefit–effort ratio, will lead to one government being able to provide more public services per head for a given tax rate than another; and this he regards as a prime case of inequity.[3]

In order to decide whether differences in benefit–effort ratios are inequitable according to our definition, it is necessary first to determine the factors causing the differences, and then to decide whether these are beyond a local government's control. The first factor, which would lead to one government providing a lower level of public services for the same effort as another, is a lower per capita tax base. If a government was equal in all respects to another except that it had a lower tax base per head, then it could not raise as much revenue for a given tax rate and hence could not provide as many services. A second factor is the existence of differences in the costs per unit of public services. If these were higher in one government than in another, then even if the first government had the same tax base, was taxing at the same rate and was in receipt of the same amount of outside revenue, it could not provide the same level of public services, simply because its costs were higher. The final factor influencing the services provided for a given tax rate is the government's savings position. If one government is saving more from its revenue than another, identical in all other respects, then if their revenues are the same it must necessarily be providing fewer public services.

The influence of these factors on the benefit–effort ratio can be demonstrated algebraically. From assumptions (a), (b) and (e), the ratio of public services per head (B_i) to tax effort (E_i) is given by:

$$\frac{B_i}{E_i} = \frac{L_i/P_i}{E_i} = \frac{T_i - A_i}{E_i P_i} = \frac{Y_i}{P_i} - \frac{A_i}{E_i P_i}$$

from which it can be seen that for a given level of E_i differences in the ratio will result from differences in the per capita tax base, Y_i, costs per unit, P_i, and the net per capita savings position, A_i.

Which of these are beyond local government control? In the situation specified by the assumptions, they all are, with the exception of A_i. From assumption (c), costs and per capita tax bases are fixed. Hence if local governments had to balance their budget (so that $A_i = 0$ for all i), differences in benefit–effort ratios would arise from factors beyond local control and could be considered inequitable.

However, neither in the world specified by our assumptions nor in fact do local governments have to balance their budget. The fact that they can save, dis-save and borrow means that they can affect the size of their benefit–effort ratio by their own decisions (at the extreme, for instance, a local government which saved all of its current revenue would have a benefit–effort ratio of zero). Thus, by saving more out of its revenue, a local government could increase the grant to which it was entitled under a programme designed to equalize benefit–effort ratios. This would lead to distortions in local savings/expenditure decisions, and would not be a desirable feature of an intergovernmental grants programme.

This disadvantage can be overcome if the benefit–effort ratio is replaced as an index of inequity by a modification that can be termed the purchasing power/effort ratio or PPE ratio. The purchasing power of a local government is the amount of public services that can be provided to local residents out of its total revenue. Under our assumptions the per capita purchasing power is T_i/P_i, and the PPE ratio is therefore:

$$\frac{T_i}{E_iP_i} = \frac{E_iY_i}{E_iP_i} = \frac{Y_i}{P_i}$$

from which it can be seen that the ratio for a given E_i will vary with differences in per capita tax base and differences in the cost per unit of public services. The level of savings of the local government is irrelevant to the determination of the PPE ratio, which would therefore seem to be a superior index of inequity to the original benefit–effort ratio.

The formula for use in a grants programme designed to equalize PPE ratios can be determined as follows. The effect of the receipt of a grant is to increase the local government's total revenue for a given effort by the real value of the grant. Thus, if the per capita money value of the grant is denoted G_i, the PPE ratio after receipt of the grant (the post-grant PPE ratio) is given by:

$$\frac{T_i + G_i}{E_iP_i} = \frac{Y_i}{P_i} + \frac{G_i}{E_iP_i}$$

Suppose the grant is used to equalize the post-grant PPE ratio to that of a 'target' government (which could be the government with the highest ratio, the median ratio or whatever). If the value of the variables for the target government is denoted by the subscript t, then its PPE ratio is:

$$\frac{T_t}{P_t E_t} = \frac{Y_t}{P_t}$$

Setting the post-grant PPE ratio equal to the PPE ratio of the target government yields the required value for G_i, that is:

$$G_i = E_i P_i \left[\frac{Y_t}{P_t} - \frac{Y_i}{P_i} \right]$$

One problem with the use of any formula such as this must be mentioned at this point. It can be seen that the grant varies with the local government's tax rate and hence is open-ended. The effect of open-ended formulae is to lower the cost to local governments of public expenditure compared with that of private expenditure. Local governments in receipt of such a grant would therefore have an incentive to increase public expenditure – a feature of the scheme that may not appeal to the budgetary agents of the central government.

To overcome this, a different type of grant structure has been suggested, under which the central government determines a standard level of either expenditure or public services and compensates local governments for disparities in their ability to provide it.[4] Under this scheme the grant awarded to each local government per head of its population would equal the difference between the expenditure per head that would be incurred if average levels of services per head were provided at average cost and the revenue per head that would be raised by applying the average tax rate to the local per capita tax base. Thus, if averages are noted by asterisks, the grant per head is equal to:

$$P^* B^* - E^* Y_i$$

Use of this or a similar formula would have the advantage that the amount of the grant received by a local government would not vary with its fiscal operations. The grant would thus not be open-ended. Regrettably, however, its use would not eliminate inequity as it has been defined here, except in the special case where all governments chose to tax at the average rate, E^*, and all had the same costs, equal to the average P^*. In that case, their PPE ratios would be identical. However, this would not be so in any other circumstances. Because the grant does not vary with the tax rate or with differences in costs, a local government in receipt of the grant with a tax rate higher (lower) than E^*, or with costs higher (lower) than P^*, would have a lower (higher) ratio than one at the average in each case. Hence, differences in PPE ratios and, therefore, inequity would still persist.

Open-endedness thus seems to be a necessary feature of a formula designed to achieve PPE equalization. But this is not the only problem associated with the scheme. The conclusion that such equalization would eliminate inequity between local governments was derived only within the context of a world in which assumptions (a)–(f) hold. The realism of these assumptions, and the implications for the analysis if they are relaxed, must now be considered.

Relaxation of assumptions

Assumption (a) – that each local government provides one public service – is clearly unrealistic, but it is not crucial to the analysis. If more than one service is provided P_i must be measured by an index of the costs of the various services. Some of the problems of obtaining such an index are discussed in the next section.

Assumption (b) – that each government only derives revenue from one tax – is also an over-simplification of the actual position, but again is not critical from a theoretical point of view. If the government also derives revenue from several taxes, then the tax base should be defined so as to include the resources from which all its revenue comes – a concept perhaps better described as its 'fiscal capacity' – and its effort should be defined as the proportion of fiscal capacity that is taken as revenue. This is also discussed further below.

By contrast, *assumption (c)* – that costs and per capita tax base (or per capita rateable value) are fixed – is critical to the analysis. For, if local governments do have control over their tax bases and their costs, then disparities in PPE ratios arise from factors within local control, and cease to be inequitable. So far as the per capita tax base is concerned, however, it seems likely that any control that governments may have, at least in the short term, is minimal: tax bases cannot be quickly raised or lowered at the whim of the local government. In the longer term, it could be argued that local governments, through the encouraging of commercial or industrial development or through the provision of services designed to appeal to high income groups, could expand their tax base if they chose. However, although undoubtedly in practice such activities do go on to a limited extent, their scope is inevitably restricted; local governments cannot expand their tax base indefinitely, not least because of the pressure of competition from other areas.

The situation with respect to costs is more complicated. In order to understand fully the factors that determine differences in costs and to assess whether they are in fact beyond local control, it is necessary to define what is meant by costs per unit of per capita public services in a more precise fashion than has been done so far. The exact definition of costs per unit in this context is discussed in the next section; hence, we postpone an assessment of the inequity of differences in costs until after that discussion.

Assumption (d) – that local services and taxes apply only to local residents and that all residents benefit equally from the services – is also unrealistic. There are services provided by the local government that benefit the residents of other governments as well as its own. Examples include the provision of through roads, the financing of a municipal museum and the provision of services for commuters who work in the government's jurisdiction but reside outside it. If the potential purchasing power for these services were included in the measure of the local government's PPE ratio, then it would over-inflate it; for we are only concerned with the relationship between public services provided for residents and the effort made by them. For instance, if a large proportion of a local government's services benefited non-residents, and if the potential to provide these benefits were included in the measure, then the government would only receive a small grant under a PPE equalization scheme – even if its own residents, who make all the effort and receive relatively little benefit, have a low 'own' PPE ratio. Accordingly, these spill-over benefits should be excluded from the measure.

Two points should be noted here. First, it should be recalled that we are only concerned with equity and not with considerations of efficiency. The latter would require that, if spill-overs exist such that the marginal national benefit of a local authority's activity is greater than the marginal local benefit, then the local authority should receive a grant sufficient to induce it to increase the level of the activity up to the point at which marginal national benefit equals marginal national cost. This would be independent of any PPE equalization grant.

Secondly, this argument rests on the assumption that local authority expenditure on non-residents in no way benefits residents. However, in some cases, such as resort towns, the residents may benefit indirectly via the multiplier effects of non-residents' expenditure on employment and income in the area. If a certain portion of the authorities' expenditure

on non-residents can be positively identified as having multiplier effects in this way, then ideally that portion should be
included in the measure of benefits.

Another type of spill-over arises from the presence of
commercial or industrial units within an area. The provision
of public services to commercial organizations benefits, in
some combination, the owner(s) of the organization, its
employees, and the consumers of whatever commodity it
produces. Residents of the local area only benefit in so far as
they fall into one of these categories. Similarly, the taxes
paid by the organization are not paid directly by residents
but by owners, employees and/or consumers. Hence some
portions of both benefit and effort are external to the area
and again strictly should not be included in the measure
(although, again, there are likely to be employment and
income effects that should be taken into account).

The other part of assumption (d) – that all residents
benefit equally – is also unrealistic. Families with children
clearly benefit more from local expenditure on education
than families without, for example. Inequities caused by
unequal distribution of public services within a government,
however, are beyond the scope of an analysis dealing with
grants between governments. All that can be done here is
simply to acknowledge that, if differences in the composition
and distribution of public services within a local government
area are regarded as inequitable, then a PPE equalization
scheme (total or discretionary) will do nothing to eliminate
this particular source of inequity.

Assumption (e) – that a local government's total revenue
equals the sum of its expenditure and net savings – is true
by definition, and therefore need not be considered further.
On the other hand, *assumption (f)* – that all local governments are free to vary their public services as they choose –
is far from realistic, and its relaxation presents considerable
difficulties for the analysis.

Assumption (f) yields the implication that differences in

per capita levels of public services arise in part from differences in community preferences and, hence, were matters of local choice. But in fact not all differences in local services can be ascribed to differences in preferences, costs or tax bases. There are also differences in the *needs* for local spending that have to be taken into account.

The concept of need is a difficult one to define in the local government context, and I do not propose to discuss it here (for an extensive treatment, see Bramley, 1990). Rather, I shall simply define local expenditure need as the expenditures necessary to provide minimum levels of certain services that are required by external factors, such as the statutory requirements of central government. These might include, for example, the maintenance of roads up to a minimum standard, the provision of schools and other educational facilities, or making available welfare services for elderly people up to a required minimum. A local government with a large quantity of such required expenditures (for example, with a large number of old people, or children of school age) is likely to 'need' a higher level of public expenditure than one with a smaller quantity; and, therefore, because of factors beyond its control, it is likely to have a higher revenue requirement.

The existence of required expenditure of this kind introduces a further source of inequity.[5] For, out of two governments with the same overall PPE ratio, one may be able to purchase fewer optional or discretionary services for the same effort than the other, simply because it has a higher burden of required services to provide from its budget. Or, if two governments were providing the same levels of discretionary services, but one had a higher level of required services, the latter would have to make a greater effort than the other. More generally, in view of the important differences in circumstances between local governments, required expenditures per head may differ substantially from government to government and, hence, create significant disparities in the ratio of local effort to local purchasing power of discretionary services. Since by definition these disparities arise from factors beyond local control, they would therefore seem to be inequitable, and the grant structure should be modified in order to eliminate them.

This can be achieved by the introduction of a variant of the basic PPE ratio: the 'discretionary' PPE ratio. This is the ratio of the amount of purchasing power per head of population available for optional or discretionary services after the required services have been provided to local effort; it is given by the expression:

$$\frac{T_i - P_i \bar{B}_i}{P_i E_i}$$

where $\bar{B}_i$ is the level of required services per head and E_i, T_i and P_i are, as before, the tax rate, tax revenue per head, and the cost per unit of public services respectively. Equalization of this ratio will result in every local government having the same discretionary purchasing power per unit effort, and hence the elimination of this source of inequity.

We have now a basic index of inequity – the 'total' PPE ratio – and a modification of the index if it is desired to take into account inequities resulting from 'needs' or required expenditures – the 'discretionary' PPE ratio. The basic formula for use in a grants programme designed to equalize discretionary PPE ratios can be obtained in a similar manner to that used above to obtain the formula for equalizing total PPE ratios. The post-grant discretionary PPE ratio for the ith government is given by:

$$\frac{T_i + G_i - P_i \bar{B}_i}{P_i E_i} \tag{8.1}$$

and the discretionary PPE ratio for the target local government is given by:

$$\frac{T_t - P_t \bar{B}_t}{P_t E_t} \qquad (8.2)$$

Setting (8.1) equal to (8.2) gives the necessary formula for G_i, that is:

$$G_i = E_i \left[\frac{P_i}{P_t} Y_t - Y_i + \frac{P_i \bar{B}_i}{E_i} - \frac{P_i \bar{B}_i}{E_t} \right] \qquad (8.3)$$

It is perhaps easier to comprehend precisely what the use of formula (8.3) would achieve if it is split into two components:

$$G_i^r = E_i \cdot P_i \left[\frac{Y_t}{P_t} - \frac{Y_i}{P_i} \right] \qquad (8.3a)$$

$$G_i^n = E_i \cdot P_i \left[\frac{\bar{B}_i}{E_i} - \frac{\bar{B}_t}{E_t} \right] \qquad (8.3b)$$

where $G_i^r + G_i^n = G_i$.

Equation (8.3a) is the basic formula for equalizing total PPE ratios and hence could be interpreted as providing compensation for differing per capita real resources.[6] (8.3b) equalizes the ratio of what might be termed the per capita 'burden of required services' to effort and, hence, could be interpreted as providing compensation for different per capita required expenditures (or needs).[7] A government receiving grants (8.3a) and (8.3b) would have both the same discretionary PPE ratio, and the same burden of required services to effort ratio, as the target.

Finally, *assumption (g)* – that there is no fiscally induced migration – is crucial to the analysis. As has been pointed out by several authors (see, for example, Bramley 1990, p. 6), if people can migrate freely from one area to another, then the case in terms of equity for intergovernmental grants is seriously weakened. If migration is costless, then, even if a local government has little control over its PPE ratio, its residents do, in the sense that they can cease to be its residents if they so choose.

However, the ties of jobs, family and community mean that in most cases migration has substantial costs. In practice, therefore, people do face restricted choices and the equity of their fiscal situation becomes relevant. Further, even if they could meet the costs of migration, there is a normative question, on both equity and efficiency grounds, concerning whether people should be forced to incur those costs by arbitrary fiscal disparities. Costly migration is not a desirable solution to the problem of fiscal inequity.

Some measurement issues

In order to implement formula (8.3) it is necessary to have measures of fiscal capacity (Y_i, Y_t), effort (E_i, E_t), the costs per unit of public services (P_i, P_t) and of the 'required' services ($\bar{B}_i$, $\bar{B}_t$). Because the definition of these concepts is not always clear and because they have to be defined before they can be measured, it is necessary to discuss precisely what is meant by them in this context. This will have the additional benefit of clarifying the way in which different circumstances and behaviour among local governments will lead to differences in costs and required services, and, in the case of costs, which of these differences should be considered inequitable.

Fiscal capacity

At first sight the measurement of fiscal capacity might seem relatively easy: the base of the tax or taxes actually used by the government in question. Thus, if the local government used only a property tax, then the appropriate measure would be the aggregate value of all the property in the area; if it only used a sales tax, then it would be the aggregate value of sales in the area.

However, in many cases the situation is not quite so simple. What if, as in the United States for example, the governments concerned derive revenue from several taxes? Simple aggregation of the relevant tax bases is unlikely to be appropriate; for it may involve extensive double-counting. What if a substantial portion of revenue comes from charges levied for services? Or what if revenue is raised by a poll tax, such as the United Kingdom's 'community charge'? More fundamentally, why should the measure of fiscal capacity depend on the choice of one particular local revenue structure over another: a choice that may be at least partly under the control of the local government concerned?

The theoretical answer to these questions is to adopt some broader concept of fiscal capacity that incorporates all the economic resources from which the local government could derive revenue. This could include a comprehensive measure of income received by each resident and of the income produced in the area by the people working in it. Practical difficulties of collecting the relevant information could preclude such an 'ideal' solution; and in that case it may be necessary to base the measure where possible on the actual tax base, modified to take account of some of the problems involved. There is not the space here to discuss the ways in which this might be done; more developed treatments of the relevant issues can be found in D. King (1984, pp. 175–8) and Foster *et al.* (1980, pp. 243–4).

Effort

As with fiscal capacity, at first sight the measurement of

effort might seem reasonably simple: the revenue raised by the local government expressed as a proportion of its fiscal capacity. However, again there are problems in practice, particularly if several taxes are levied and if fiscal capacity is measured in relation to the relevant tax bases.

More fundamentally, as Aronson (1977) has pointed out in a comment on the original discussion of PPE equalization, there is a difficulty with focusing on *fiscal* effort alone. For this may penalize local communities who decide to provide services through the private sector rather than the public sector. Even if fiscal PPE ratios are equalized, inequalities in private purchasing power will still exist; and therefore inequalities in 'private' PPE ratios will continue.

The difficulty with this line of argument is that, taken to its logical conclusion, it implies the full equalization of all local economic resources (Le Grand, 1977). This has enormous economic and philosophical implications that are likely to be unacceptable. As with the measurement of fiscal capacity, therefore, to overcome these problems in practice, it may be necessary to adopt some less than ideal solution, such as those based on a modified version of tax effort discussed in D. King (1984, pp. 178–9).

Costs per unit

There are two problems in trying to find a measure of the cost per unit of all public services in a local government: that of finding a definition and measure for each individual service, and that of integrating the measures for each service to form a single cost index. Of these, the more important is the definition of costs per unit for a particular service, and it is on this that I concentrate here.

In any attempt to define the costs per unit of a public service it is useful to distinguish between the 'output' level of the service and the 'inputs' that go into producing that output. By output in this context is meant the aspect of the service that provides direct benefit to the individual (that is, the argument in her utility function). By input is meant the various factors of production that are combined to produce the output. The local government is thus being viewed as a producer of public services, combining input factors to produce outputs that provide utility to consumers.

As an example of the application of this distinction, consider the case of education. Output here – the factor from which consumers derive utility – might be defined as the total bundle of educational skills acquired by schoolchildren (as measured by, for example, examination results). The inputs, on the other hand, would be the number of teachers, classrooms, teaching aids, etc. Or consider police services. The output in this case might be the reduction in the probability of having a given crime committed against a given person; the inputs would be the number of policemen, patrol cars, radio communication equipment, etc.

Now it should be clear that, for the purpose of PPE equalization, it is output that is the relevant measure of the public service and not its inputs. It is differences in local governments' ability to purchase benefits for their residents with which we are concerned; differences in their ability to purchase inputs are only of interest in so far as they affect differences in ability to purchase output. Hence, the first conclusion is that the measure of cost that is required is cost per unit output of public services and not cost per unit input.

More formally, the relationship between outputs, inputs and their respective costs per unit can be summarized by equation (8.4). There are assumed to be m factors of production, whose quantities employed by the ith local government per head of its population in production of the jth service are denoted by $F_{ij}^k (k = 1, ..., m)$, and whose price per unit by W_{ij}^k (which may be the same for all services). B_{ij} is the per capita output of the jth service in the ith government, and

P_{ij} the unit cost of per capita output:

$$P_{ij} \cdot B_{ij} = \sum_{k=1}^{m} W_{ij}^{k} \cdot F_{ij}^{k}. \tag{8.4}$$

(8.4) is simply a budget equation, requiring that the total cost of providing the service equals total expenditure upon inputs. It can thus be viewed as a definitional equation for P_{ij}: the correct definition of costs per unit for PPE equalization purposes.

How can P_{ij} be measured? This would depend on obtaining a satisfactory measure of B_{ij}. If, for example, it were considered that the total number of examination results achieved was a satisfactory measure of educational output, and if data on this were obtainable at a local level, then P_{ij} for education could be measured by dividing this number into the total local expenditure on education per head of total population. Or, if the average road speed per journey were considered the best measure of output of the services of roads provided by a local government, then this figure could be divided into local per capita expenditure on roads to obtain P_{ij} for roads.

We must now consider briefly the problem of aggregation. Even if estimates of P_{ij}'s can be obtained, it is necessary to combine them in some way to form P_i, that is, the cost index for use in formula (8.3). Here again there are difficulties. Construction of indices requires the adoption of a system to weight the different components, and agreement has to be reached on the appropriate method of doing so. The most obvious weight for each P_{ij} is the proportion of a local government's total expenditure that is spent on service j. However, this would be unsatisfactory from the point of view of PPE equalization, because those proportions are under the control of local governments and, hence, the value of the index P_i would be influenced by factors subject to local control. Perhaps the best way to overcome this problem is to use the national average proportion of total local expenditure, which is spent on service j as a weight. But whatever system is finally chosen, care would have to be taken that each local government is convinced that the system is fair to it, otherwise considerable political obstacles might be raised.

Inequity and costs per unit

We are now in a position to resume the discussion of the relationship between cost differences and inequity that was deferred from the previous section. Specifically, it is necessary to examine the factors that determine differences in P_{ij} in order to assess the degree to which they are beyond local control. The principal factors determining any P_{ij} will be (i) input factor prices, (ii) the type of the production functions for the jth service in the ith government, and (iii) the degree to which the local government acts as a cost minimizer (its 'efficiency'). Thus, *ceteris paribus*, from (8.4) changes in factor prices will lead to changes in expenditure upon input factors (both directly and via any effects on the quantities of inputs employed), so leading to changes in costs per unit output. Local governments with different production functions will be able to produce different levels of output from the same combinations of inputs and, hence, incur different costs per unit output. Given a set of factor prices and its production function, the costs of a local government will depend on its efficiency: its ability to reduce the cost per unit of a given output.[8]

Casual empirical observation would suggest that the degree of control that local governments can exercise over input prices is small. On the whole, local governments have to take as given the wages they have to pay, the prices of raw material, land, and capital equipment they use, and the fees of the sub-contractors they employ. These all tend to be determined by market or other factors operating regionally or nationally, and are not generally amenable to local government direction. Hence, differences in costs per unit that arise from different input prices do seem to be beyond local control and are therefore inequitable.

What causes differences in local government production functions – differences in the outputs of (equally efficient) local governments from a given combination of inputs? Generally, what might be termed differences in circumstances. These circumstances might be geographical: the larger the area of a government, the more the necessary inputs into police services to obtain a given level of police protection. They may be demographic: the greater the population density (and hence traffic congestion) the lower the output of refuse disposal services (as measured by, for example, the number of collections per year) for given inputs. Or they may be social: because of the influence of home background, the higher the proportion of middle-class pupils in a school, the greater might be the educational output of that school for a given set of inputs. All of these circumstances – geographic, demographic and social – are likely to be largely beyond the control of the government; hence, in so far as they contribute to differences in costs per unit output, they too should be regarded as sources of inequity.

However, the same cannot be said for the third determinant of differences in costs: the efficiency of the local government in production. To the degree to which it does not minimize costs within the constraints of its production function and input factor prices, a local government can be said to be inefficient: and this is clearly a matter that is within its control. Differences in costs that arise from differences in efficiency are thus not sources of inequity, and hence should not be compensated for.

This suggests that the value of P_{ij} used in the grant formula should not be a government's *actual* costs per unit, but its *potential* costs: the value that would pertain if the government successfully minimized costs. This potential cost per unit would be determined only by differences in factor prices and in production functions and, therefore, only by factors beyond local control. In practice, however, this would be a very difficult figure to obtain for each government; a more practical procedure might be to use the actual value of costs per unit for most governments and only to undertake some downward adjustment in cases where conclusive evidence was available that a local government was inefficient.

Needs

There are two types of need that require service expenditure. The first includes those statutorily required by the central government. These may take the form of 'output' requirements (i.e. requiring a minimum B_{ij}) or of 'input' requirements (i.e. requiring a minimum of F_{ij}^k). Examples of the former include requirements for educational standards to be above a certain level; examples of the latter include requirements that classrooms should not be less than a certain size, etc. In the first case, the problem of finding a measure is part of the more general problem of finding a measure of output. In the second case, if minimum levels of F_{ij}^k are fixed for all k, then this implies a minimum level of B_{ij}; and measurement of this would require, in addition to a measure of output, knowledge of each local government's production function. So in neither case would the measure be easy to obtain.

The other category of required services presents a further difficulty in addition to that of defining output. The category is perhaps best considered as comprising those services that the local government is under some compulsion to provide, at least up to a minimum level. This might include services that some local governments have to provide while others do not (e.g. protection against sea erosion). Alternatively, it might include services that all governments provide, but which they are under moral pressure to supply at least up to a certain minimum (e.g. refuse disposal). The problem is that the degree to which the choice of a local government is restricted by outside pressure is extremely difficult, if not impossible, to assess (even in the case of statutorily required services it could be argued that local authorities do have a choice because, if they are prepared to face the consequences, they have the possibility of non-compliance).

The decision as to which services fall into this category must therefore almost inevitably be a subjective one. My own preference would be to include only those services that arise from very obvious differences in circumstances, such as sea erosion, and not to include services provided by all governments, since in these cases the levels of provision above the statutory minimum do seem to be the results of local choice.

Finally, the problem of aggregation. This is less severe than in the case of costs, because formula (8.3) can be adapted quite simply to allow for there being more than one required service. If there are, say, s services for which some minimum level is required then $P_i \bar{B}_i$ in formula (8.3) should be replaced respectively by:

$$\sum_{j=1}^{s} P_{ij}\bar{B}_{ij} \text{ and } \frac{P_i}{P_t} \sum_{j=1}^{s} P_{tj}\bar{B}_{tj}$$

This will still result in the equalization of the ith government's discretionary PPE ratio to that of the target.

Conclusion

This chapter has attempted to identify some of the principal sources of inequity between local governments' fiscal operations and to provide some suggestions for the theoretical formulation of a grants scheme to reduce or eliminate them. A fiscal disparity was defined as inequitable if it arose from factors beyond local control. It was argued that a suitable indicator of inequity was the ratio of a local government's real purchasing power to its tax rate or effort – the (total) PPE ratio. If two governments had different PPE ratios, then one could purchase more public services for a given effort than the other. It was shown that differences in PPE ratios arose from differences in tax bases per head, and in costs per unit output (likely to be considerable because of the very differing circumstances of differing local governments). These were indeed factors largely beyond local control, and hence differences in PPE ratios could be considered inequitable. A further complication was introduced by the existence of local services that were not under local control: 'required' services. Differences in these created disparities in the ratio of the 'discretionary' purchasing power of local governments to their effort – the discretionary PPE ratio – and these also could be judged inequitable. Formulae were presented for achieving the equalization of total and discretionary PPE ratios.

There is little new in the identification of the principal sources of inequity. The basic items considered – fiscal capacities, costs, and required services or 'needs' – have long been considered as potential causes of injustice, and most intergovernmental grant systems go some way towards compensating governments badly off in these respects. What has been done here is to use the arguments of previous chapters to provide a rationale for the identification of disparities in those factors as inequitable, and, by modifying Thurow's contribution of the benefit–effort ratio, to provide a specific objective for a grants programme aimed at eliminating the inequity caused by these disparities: the equalization of (total or discretionary) PPE ratios.

Notes: Chapter 8

1   Sources: for the UK, United Kingdom Treasury (1990, ch. 21.4); for the other countries, D. King (1984, p. 185, Table 5.2).

2 This is illustrated in the voluminous literature on the topic. The pioneers include Sydney Webb (1920) and J. R. and Ursula Hicks (1943). More recent contributions include Buchanan (1950, 1952), Musgrave (1961), Boyle (1966), Thurow (1970), Bradford and Oates (1971), Le Grand and Reschovsky (1971), Godley and Rhodes (1973), Foster *et al.* (1980), Oates (1982), D. King (1984) and Bramley (1990). This chapter is a development of the arguments in Le Grand (1975a, 1977).

3 For further discussion of the benefit–effort ratio and its implications for revenue sharing in the United States, see Le Grand and Reschovsky (1971).

4 See, for example, Hicks and Hicks (1943), Boyle (1966, pp. 34–6) and Godley and Rhodes (1973).

5 I am indebted to David Champernowne for pointing out the difficulties with an earlier formulation of this argument and for the provision of the formula (8.3b).

6 More accurately, it removes differences in total PPE ratios, excluding those due to receipt of G_i^n. Thus substitution of (8.3a) into the expression $(T_i + G_i^n)/P_i.E_i$ yields Y_t/P_t, which is equal to the target authority's total PPE ratio.

7 If the 'burden of required services' is defined as the difference between the real value of the expenditure on required services and the real value of any grant received to compensate for those services, then the ratio of this burden to effort is given by $(P_i\bar{B}_i - G_i^n)/(P_iE_i)$. Substitution of (8.3b) into this reduces it to $\bar{B}_t/E_t$, that is, the per capita burden of required services to effort ratio of the target authority.

8 This should include its ability to take account of economies of scale by, for example, combining with other authorities for the provision of certain services.

9 Equity, the measurement of choice sets and income taxation

The conception of equity discussed in earlier chapters provides a criterion for judging whether a given distribution of resources is equitable or not. As long as preferences are regarded as autonomous, a distribution will be inequitable if it is the outcome of each individual making choices over unequal choice sets; it will be equitable if every individual faces the same choice set. It has been argued that this interpretation captures a major part of the way the term is commonly applied to distributional issues.

But, whatever its abstract merits, this definition on its own will be of little use for many policy purposes. In particular, it will never be feasible to create a situation where each individual's choice set is equal to that of every other individual. Even if it were feasible, it would not be desirable, given the sacrifices of other values that would have to be made to achieve such a utopian end.

Therefore, the decisions that are likely to confront policy-makers who are concerned with equity and who accept the choice-related interpretation of the concept will involve comparing situations where individuals have different choice sets. They may need simply to rank such situations, according the degree of inequity present; but, more likely, they will need actually to measure in some way the extent of inequity in such situations. This in turn will require measuring the 'size' of the disparities between individuals' choice sets: a task which, among other things, will require measuring the size of the choice sets themselves.

The proper development of techniques for measuring the size of choice sets is an enormous task and one beyond the scope of a book chapter. Instead, the chapter has the more modest intention of drawing attention to some of the difficulties involved in measuring choice sets for particular policy purposes and of suggesting ways in which they might be resolved. To focus the argument, it concentrates on an instrument that is crucial to most discussions of redistribution policy: that of income taxation. Many of the issues involved are somewhat technical; in consequence, much of the analysis will only be accessible to specialists.

The first section of the chapter is a discussion of the properties that it would be desirable for measures of choice sets to possess for the purposes of income taxation. The second investigates whether existing or proposed measures possess these properties. Again, the exigencies of space mean that the discussion has had to be limited; so it focuses on the particular problems created by nonlinearities in the budget constraint. The third section discusses some alternative measures, ones that do have the desired properties. The final section offers some brief concluding reflections concerning the economic analysis of choice sets as compared with that of utility functions.

Choice sets and income taxation

Equity considerations loom large in the formulation of income tax policy. This is not surprising; income taxes reduce people's command over economic resources, and any attempt to change the extent of the latter will have to be seen to be equitable or fair to be acceptable. Hence, it is necessary for any measure of income that is used for income tax purposes also to be regarded as equitable.

What are the properties that an equitable income measure should possess? Of the many possible such properties there is one of particular importance, given the arguments of this book. It is that the measure should be related to the individual's choice set and not to her autonomous preferences. That is, it should not depend on, for example, an individual's relative preferences for commodities and leisure, or on her relative preferences for present and future consumption. Differences in the measure should reflect only differences in the choice sets that the relevant individuals face, not differences in their (autonomous) tastes.

The desirability of such a property arises in part from the concept of income itself; for this conventionally refers to the constraints within which people exercise their preferences and which bound the choice set. But it can also be justified by the interpretation of equity relating the concept to individual choice, as discussed in earlier chapters.

The relevance of this conception to the taxation issue can perhaps be most easily motivated by reference to two simple examples (versions of which will be instantly recognizable to any student of public finance). Suppose there is an income tax, the exact details of which are unimportant except that (a) those on higher incomes pay more tax than those on low incomes and (b) income is measured by money income. First, consider an atemporal example of labour supply, where there are two working individuals who are identical in all respects (including their ability, their wage rate and the time they have available for work) except that, for any given amount of leisure, one has a lower marginal rate of substitution of money income for leisure than the other. They thus have identical choice sets; but, *ceteris paribus*, the former will consume more leisure than the latter and therefore have a lower money income. Under the tax system, she will therefore pay less tax: an outcome that, given the basic identity of their situations, does not seem horizontally equitable.

The second example concerns two individuals making savings decisions over two periods. Each individual receives the same value of exogenous income in the first period, and none in the second; each faces the same interest rate. The individuals are also identical in every other respect, except that one has a lower marginal rate of substitution of present for future consumption than the other. Again, the choice sets are identical; but, *ceteris paribus*, the former will save more than the latter and hence have a larger income in the second period. Both will pay the same tax in the first period, but the 'saver' will pay more tax in the second period than the 'spender'. Thus, the saver will pay more tax over her life-time than the spender. Again, this seems an inequitable outcome.

These examples are, of course, illustrations of two more wide-ranging debates concerning the equity of income tax systems: one concerning the omission of leisure from the tax base, and the other, the so-called double taxation of savings. This is not the place to enter extensively into these debates. For our purposes, it is sufficient to point out that, in each case, the problem appears to arise because observed differences in money incomes could reflect as much differences in preferences as differences in constraints; and to conclude that it would therefore be preferable from the point of view of equity to use an income measure for the tax base that was independent of preferences – if such can be found.

There is a further, practical reason why it is convenient to ignore differences in preferences when constructing policy. It is that, if such differences are considered to be relevant to policy, it is likely that at some point they will have to be identified and compared. Although, in simple cases, it may be possible to rely solely on observed behaviour, this becomes progressively more difficult once situations become more complex. The only alternative is explicitly to postulate utility functions that are interpersonally comparable and take on a particular functional form, a requirement to be avoided if at all possible, given the well-known difficulties involved. [1]

The desirability of preference independence, at least from an equity point of view, leads to two more specific properties. The first is that the value of the measure should be the same for individuals with identical choice sets. This can be interpreted as a form of horizontal equity. This in turn has the vertical equity corollary that if one individual has a larger (smaller) choice set than another, then the measure should rank the first individual above (below) the other. We shall discuss below a range of possible interpretations for the terms larger or smaller in this context; but, for the moment, it is sufficient to interpret them strictly as referring to whether one set is a subset of another. More specifically, the measure should rank an individual whose choice set is a subset of another individual below that individual.

It will aid the subsequent discussion if these requirements are put more formally. Let S and T be two choice sets. Then a measure of income $I(\ )$ is required such that:

$$I(S) = I(T) \text{ if } S = T \qquad \text{(HE)}$$

and that:

$$I(S) > I(T) \text{ whenever } S \supset T \qquad \text{(VE)}$$

The first of these may be termed a *Horizontal Equity (HE) Axiom*, and the second a *Vertical Equity (VE) Axiom*. Their requirements seem relatively mild; yet, as we shall see, it is surprising how many simple measures of choice sets violate them.

Of course, neither these properties, nor the more general concerns of equity that they reflect, are the only considerations that should affect the choice of an income measure for taxation purposes. Although this discussion is primarily concerned with equity criteria, for that is the focus of the book, other considerations will be mentioned where appropriate.

Measures of choice sets

In searching for a measure consistent with the choice-based interpretation of equity, the fact that the focus of concern is with the choices open to individuals suggests that it might be fruitful to focus on the elements of the choice set. Alternatively, since the range of choices is determined by constraint parameters, it may be preferable to focus on those parameters; that is, to specify a functional relationship between the parameters that has the desired properties and, ideally, has a sensible economic interpretation.

To start with measures that focus on the elements of the choice set: a number of writers have discussed these, including, notably, Sen (1985).[2] As was discussed in Chapter 6, Sen is concerned with ranking sets defined over 'functionings' rather than commodities; but this does not affect this particular argument. He posits what is termed a 'valuation' function: a function particular to each individual that attaches a scalar value to each particular set of functionings. This function is employed in devising possible ways of ranking different sets. One method is to use the value of the best element in each set to rank it (Sen 1985, p. 61). This has the problem that widening of the set without affecting the 'best value' has no effect on the measure; it thus does not have the VE property. As an alternative, Sen suggests incorporating the extent in the measure, as measured by the number of elements in the set. In that case, one set would be ranked above another if both the marginal value of the best element were greater, *and* if it contained at least as many elements (Sen 1985, p. 68).

But this measure also does not have all the required properties. In particular, although Sen is careful to distinguish the valuation function from a utility function, it shares the property of the latter of being (at least partly) subjective. It is therefore dependent on 'preferences' (defined in the widest possible sense), and hence any measure based on it will violate the HE axiom.

This problem could be resolved by dropping the valuation element in the two-parameter characterization. The size of the set would then depend simply on the number of its elements. This would be consistent with both axioms. But the procedure involves giving equal weight to each combination, which might seem peculiar; for instance, combinations that were not on the budget line (and hence that would not be chosen by a rational individual) would be given an equal weight to those that were. This could be overcome by confining the summation to the number of combinations along the budget line. Further, if it was necessary to give the index a money value, the combinations could be priced prior to summation by the prices prevailing along the line.

But 'counting' procedures of these kinds, in whatever form they take, are rather unconventional, to say the least. More seriously, they depend crucially on there being an observable and finite number of feasible bundles to be counted: a requirement that seems unlikely to be generally fulfilled. An alternative, more in line with conventional thinking, is to focus, not on the elements of the set, but on the parameters that determine the boundaries of the set. The problem then becomes one of specifying a functional relationship between those parameters that yields a scalar measure with the desired properties.

If all the elements over which the choices can be exercised have prices attached to them, and if all individuals face the same prices, then one measure is simply the value of each individual's budget constraint: that is, the money value of the individual's exogenous resources. If budget constraints are linear, then this measure has the properties specified in the HE and VE axioms. Individuals with resources of equal money value will have identical choice sets; individuals with resources of a higher (lower) money value than others will have larger (smaller) choice sets.

However, problems arise with this measure if there are commodities that cannot be purchased at a price, if individuals do not face the same prices and if budget constraints are nonlinear. If some commodities cannot be purchased, then an individual's resources cannot be exchanged for those commodities and hence they do not have a value with respect to those commodities. If individuals face different sets of prices, then, even if they have the same money value of resources, the 'real' value of those resources and thus the choices open to them will be different, and the HE property will be violated. This could be overcome by the use of a price index to determine for each individual the real value of her income. However, this index would have to be constructed without reference to the individual's preferences.

The problems created by nonlinear budget constraints are less obvious, and therefore need a more detailed exposition; this will occupy most of the rest of this chapter. They occur in the context of both capital and labour markets, and it will be convenient to treat these separately, at least to begin with.

Nonlinearities in capital markets

Nonlinearities in the relevant budget constraints for individuals operating in capital markets occur for a wide variety of reasons, including transactions costs, uncertainty, transactions at non-market prices, or the intrinsic illiquidity of certain types of asset (such as human capital). So basic are some of these (such as uncertainty or the illiquidity of human capital) that it is almost impossible to imagine a

world where they did not exist; hence, it is essential that they
be properly taken into account in policy formation.

The problems these create for the construction of a
preference-independent measure of income can best be illustrated by the use of a simple example. Suppose there is one
commodity, 'consumption', with a price equal to unity that
can be consumed in period 0 (quantity, c_0) or in period 1
(c_1). An individual's utility function, u is defined over c_0 and
c_1, and is quasi-concave. Each individual receives an
exogenous income of y_0 in period 0 and y_1 in period 1.

Now suppose that there is some capital market imperfec-
tion (the exact source of which does not matter), such that
while each individual can lend at a rate r, he or she can only
borrow at a rate $\rho(\rho > r)$. This is a very common form of
nonlinearity, and hence a good example for our purposes;
however, the relevant points could easily be made by using
other examples, such as the existence of (non-human) capital
assets of varying liquidity. Assume all lending and borrowing
takes place in period 0, and all repayments in period 1.

The maximization process is formally set out in Appendix
9.1. Here we give a diagrammatic exposition. In Figure 9.1,
the situation is depicted in a standard fashion for two individuals A and B, who have different utility functions and
hence indifference maps, but who face the same constraints
(y_0, y_1, r and ρ). U_A represents the highest indifference
curve that A can attain; U_B, the highest indifference curve
that B can obtain. A is thus a lender in period 0 and B a
borrower.

Suppose a tax-and-transfer policy is introduced, the details
of which do not matter, except a central requirement that
each individual is treated equitably over their 'life-time' (the
two periods). A measure of 'life-time' income is therefore
needed that satisfies the HE and VE properties as defined
earlier.

But, for the principal measures of income found in the
literature, these properties would not generally be satisfied.

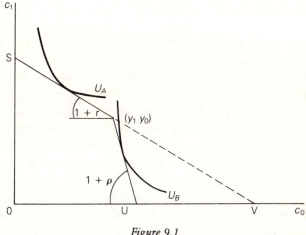

Figure 9.1

Money income clearly does not have the HE property, because, although the choice sets are equal, the level of money income in the second period is dependent on the savings and borrowings decisions of the individuals concerned. Nor does the measure that would have been appropriate in the case of a linear budget constraint: the present discounted value of the individuals' consumption-streams, or (which is the same) the present discounted value of their exogenous incomes. In A's case, this would be $y_0 + y_1/(1 + r)$, corresponding to OV on the diagram. In B's case it would be $y_0 + y_1/(1 + \rho)$, corresponding to OU on the diagram. Despite the fact that they face the same constraints, their life-time income, as measured in this way, is different.[3]

Unfortunately, the same is true of the other principal measure of life-time income, put forward by Pissarides (1978) and used by Cowell (1979). Pissarides suggests that lifetime income can be defined as exogenous income that, if it were received in the first period instead of the stream y_0, y_1, would leave the individual on the same indifference curve. He derives a formula (p. 284) for the measure, which would give a value of life-time income, I, in our notation as:

$$I = y_0 + (\lambda_1/\lambda_0)y_1 \qquad (9.1)$$

where λ_1/λ_0 is the slope of the indifference curve at the point of equilibrium and is therefore the ratio of the marginal utilities of income (λ_1, λ_0) in the relevant periods. These marginal utilities of income are functions of preferences and therefore are dependent on factors 'traditionally not regarded as arguments in the determinants of wealth' (Pissarides 1978, p. 283).

Now the Pissarides formula is not quite correct. Consider individual B. For her, the slope of the indifference curve, λ_1/λ_0, is equal to the slope of her budget constraint, $1/1 + \rho$. Therefore, from (9.1) $I = y_0 + (1/1 + \rho)y_1$. However, if she received an income equal to I in period 0, she could only lend it out at a rate of r; equilibrium would not be on the same indifference curve. This is demonstrated in Figure 9.2, where SQU represents B's 'old' budget constraint, and XU (parallel to SQ) the budget constraint she would face if she were given income in period 0 corresponding to the

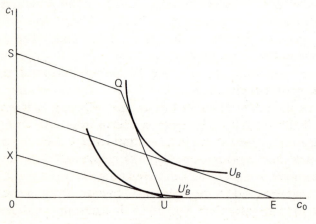

Figure 9.2

Pissarides formula. Equilibrium is now on indifference curve U_B' instead of the original curve of U_B. To be on I_B, she would need to receive an amount in period 0 equal to OE (> OU): OE is thus the correct indifference-equivalent measure of life-time income.[4]

However, although his formula is not correct, Pissarides's general point remains. There is no general formula for OE independent of the parameters of the utility function, for the value of OE will depend on the shape of the indifference curve. More generally, it is not possible to measure life-time income in the presence of non-linearities in capital markets in the fashion suggested without some reference to the parameters of the utility function: a fact that implies that the HE property is violated.[5]

Nonlinearities in labour markets

The other area where nonlinearities in budget constraints have received a great deal of attention concerns the labour supply decision. Because of such well-established features of the real world as overtime premiums, secondary earnings activities and unearned income, individuals making labour/leisure choices generally face non-linear budget constraints;[6] a fact that complicates considerably any analyses of these choices. The existence of these non-linearities make it difficult to measure individual incomes in any sensible fashion, even in a one-period world.

Again, we can illustrate this with a simple two-person example. Suppose individuals A and B both face the same standard wage rate, w, but receive an overtime premium, p, after a certain number of hours are worked, h. Their budget constraint, together with the relevant indifference curves for the two individuals, is depicted in the standard money income (y)/leisure (l) diagram, as in Figure 9.3. It will be observed that individual A's equilibrium point is within the

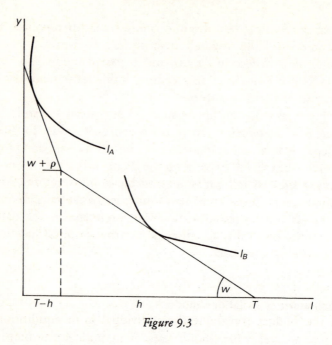

Figure 9.3

over-time section of the budget constraint, while that for B is in the standard section.

Now if $y_{a,b}$ and $l_{a,b}$ are the equilibrium values of individuals' money income and leisure respectively, and if T denotes the maximum time available for either work or leisure (assumed to be the same for both individuals), then, for A:

$$y_a = wh + (w + p)(T - h - l_a) \qquad (9.2)$$

or:

$$wh + (w + p)(T - h) = y_a + (w + p)l_a \qquad (9.3)$$

where the left-hand side is full income, equal to expenditure on goods, y_a, and on leisure, l_a, valued at the marginal wage rate, $(w + p)$. Similarly for B:

$$y_b = w(T - l_b)$$

or:

$$wT = y_b + wl_b \qquad (9.4)$$

where wT is full income.

Now we have two possible conceptions of income: money income, y_a and y_b, and full income, as given by (9.3) and (9.4). Of these, money income is clearly determined in part by individual preferences, and does not have the HE property. For this reason, the use of full income has been recommended (Taussig 1973; Musgrave 1976). But, unfortunately, the same problem arises with full income; for inspection of (9.3) and (9.4) reveals that its value depends on which part of the budget constraint the individual is in equilibrium with, upon which in turn depends her indifference map.

There is a third possible measure of income that does not suffer from this problem. That is what might be termed no-leisure income; that is, the money income that the individual would obtain if she spent all the time available on work. This corresponds to the intercept of the budget constraint with the y axis. In a world of linear budget constraints, it is the same as full income; and, in this case, it is the same as A's full income (though not the same as B's). It is identical for both individuals, and independent of preferences; it thus meets the HE property.

Unfortunately, it does not generally meet the VE property. Suppose the individuals face different budget constraints, as shown in Figure 9.4. Clearly the parameters determining the constraints are different, as are the feasible choice sets open to the individuals, with A's set being a subset of B's. Yet the value of no-leisure income is the same in both cases. Hence, the VE property is violated.

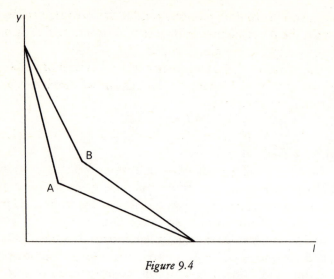

Figure 9.4

As in the capital markets' case, therefore, the various measures of income discussed are unsatisfactory, because they fail to meet the (relatively mild) requirements of the HE and VE properties. Are there alternatives that do meet both criteria? The next section discusses some possibilities.

Composite measures

A difficulty with this approach is that although, as we have seen, the commonly used scalar measures of income do violate the HE and VE properties, there is a very wide range of possible functions of the relevant parameters that do not. However, there is another property that it seems reasonable to ask the measure to satisfy and that has the effect of significantly narrowing the range. This I shall term the *Linearity Axiom*. Its exact specification will vary from case to case; and I shall shortly give the specifications that apply to the particular examples discussed here. However, the general requirement that the property codifies is relatively simple. It is that the measure should be identical to standard measures if the budget constraint is linear.

The rationale for this property will become more clear in the context of our examples. In the *capital markets* case it requires the following:

$$\text{If } y_0 = 0, \ I = y_1/1 + \rho \qquad \text{(LA1)}$$

$$\text{If } y_1 = 0, \ I = y_0 \qquad \text{(LA2)}$$

$$\text{If } \rho = r, \ I = y_0 + y_1/1 + r \qquad \text{(LA3)}$$

Each of these three conditions seems reasonable. If exogenous income in the first period is zero, so that lending is impossible, then the measure of income should simply be equal to the present value of income in the second period, discounted at the borrowing rate (LA1). If exogenous income in the second period is zero, so that borrowing is impossible, then the measure of income simply is equal to the value of exogenous income in the first period (LA2). And, if the borrowing and lending interest rates are the same, then the budget constraint is linear and the measure of income becomes the 'standard' one of the present value of exogenous income in both periods, discounted at the one interest rate (LA3).

One function that satisfies those conditions and has some other interesting properties is the CES function:

$$\left\{ \pi \left(y_0 + \frac{y_1}{1+r} \right)^{-\varepsilon} + \left(1 - \pi \right) \left(y_0 + \frac{y_1}{1+\rho} \right)^{-\varepsilon} \right\}^{-1/\varepsilon} \qquad (9.5)$$

where

$$\pi = \frac{y_0(1+r)}{y_1 + y_0(1+r)}$$

(9.5) is a weighted sum of the two measures of the present discounted value of exogenous income. The weights are related to the position of the 'kink' in the constraint. Thus the larger is y_1 relative to y_0, the longer is the 'borrowing' section of the constraint, the greater the probability that equilibrium will be on that section and the greater the weight given in the measure to the 'borrowing' measure of present discounted value. Similarly, the greater y_0 relative to y_1, the longer the 'lending' section of the budget constraint, the greater the probability that equilibrium will be on that section and the greater the weight given to the lending measure.

Another property of (9.5) can be obtained by setting $\varepsilon = 1$. Then (9.5) can be rewritten as:

$$\frac{2Q}{y_1 + y_0(1 + r)}$$

where

$$Q = y_1 y_0 + \tfrac{1}{2} y_0 \cdot y_0(1 + r) + \tfrac{1}{2} y_1 \cdot \frac{y_1}{1 + \rho}$$

and is the formula for the *area* of the choice set. This suggests that the area of a choice set might be another measure that might be suitable for our purposes.

The area as a measure has certain attractions. In particular, as a geometric representation of the size of the set, it seems to combine the parameter approach with the size approach considered earlier. However, it also has some disadvantages. A trivial one is that, as a particular monotonic transformation of (9.5), it only meets the linearity conditions if they are transformed in the same manner. More seriously, it is not easy to see how it could be readily generated over more than two periods: a problem that might limit its general usefulness.

In the *labour markets* case, the LA property imposes the requirements that:

$$\text{If } h = T, \ I = wT \tag{LA1}$$

$$\text{If } h = 0, \ I = (w + p)T \tag{LA2}$$

$$\text{If } p = 0, \ I = wT \tag{LA3}$$

These conditions are similar to those in the capital markets case, with the first two requiring that the measure I corresponds to full income if no overtime is possible (LA1), all hours are paid at overtime rates (LA2), and if there is no overtime premium (LA3).

Again a function that meets the requirements is CES of the form:

$$\left[\left(\frac{h}{T} \right) \left(wT \right)^{-\varepsilon} + \left(\frac{T-h}{T} \right) \left(wh + \{ w + p \} \{ T - h \} \right)^{-\varepsilon} \right]^{-1/\varepsilon}$$

$$\tag{9.6}$$

(9.6) corresponds to the similar expression derived in the capital markets case (9.5) and has similar properties. It is a weighted average of the full incomes of the two individuals, with the weights being related to the location of the kink in the budget constraint. The larger h, the more likely equilibrium will be found on the standard section of the constraint, and the greater the weight given to the standard measure of full income; the smaller h, the more likely equilibrium will occur on the overtime section and the greater the weight given to the overtime measure.

Again (9.6) with ε set equal to unity can be related to the area under the budget constraint. In this case (9.6) can be written as $2Q/T$ where Q is given by:

$$Q = \tfrac{1}{2} \left[hwT + (T - h)\{ wh + (w + p)(T - h)\} \right]$$

and is the formula for the area of the relevant choice set. Again this suggests that the area might be a suitable measure of the size of the constraint. Moreover, the disadvantage of the area in the capital markets' case – that it cannot easily be generalized into more than two dimensions – is perhaps less acute in this case, since non-linear budget constraints in labour markets can be commonly expressed in two dimensions.

In these simple cases, therefore, it does seem possible to construct some measures of income based on the analyses of choice sets that have the properties we seek. It does not seem as though there would be a great deal of difficulty, in principle at least, of applying some of the concepts, at least in more complex situations. Data requirements and computational complexity would doubtless increase, but these do not seem to be insurmountable problems. Too much should not be claimed on the basis of simple examples; but, at the least, what these illustrations suggest is that the examination of the parameters of choice sets may have potential as a method of resolving some of the difficulties involved in their measurement.

Conclusion

A principal aim of this chapter has been to point out some of the difficulties that non-linear budget constraints create for measures of income that might be used for constructing an equitable income tax. All the conventional measures are either partly a function of preferences or do not necessarily change in the same direction as changes in the choice set; they thus fail to have key properties that, from the point of view of the conception of equity advocated here, would seem desirable. Some alternatives, focusing on the choice set itself or on the parameters determining it have been discussed; some look more promising than others, but even those require further development.

I conclude the chapter with a reflection concerning the economic analysis of choice sets. The concept of utility has dominated welfare economics since the latter's inception. Given the difficulties of working with a metric that most economists regard as intrinsically unmeasurable, it is remarkable how far the subject has been able to develop and produce results. Yet utility-based analysis of policy inevitably has its limitations, particularly when, as so often, it necessitates unrealistic assumptions about mathematically tractable, identical and interpersonally comparable utility functions. In such cases, it may be sounder, both in theoretical and practical terms, to base policy analysis on individuals' choice sets rather than on their utilities. Choice sets are (generally) observable, they are determined by measurable parameters, and there is a respectable philosophical case for concentrating upon people's range of choices rather than on their levels of utility as a focus for policy. The difficulty is that, as indeed the previous section illustrates, the analysis of choice sets is in an exceedingly primitive state compared with that for utility. We need to discover whether the analysis can be developed in ways that can ultimately be as interesting and as fruitful as its older competitor. This chapter is a tentative step along that road.

Appendix 9.1   The capital markets model

If gross lending is denoted b and gross borrowing β, the individual's maximization problem is to maximize $u(c_0, c_1)$, subject to the budget constraints:

$$y_0 + \beta = c_0 + b \tag{9.7}$$

$$y_1 + (1+r)b = c_1 + (1+\rho)\beta \tag{9.8}$$

and the non-negativity constraints c_0, c_1, b, $\beta \geqslant 0$.

Form the function:

$$F = u(c_0, c_1) + \lambda_0(y_0 + \beta - c_0 - b)$$
$$+ \lambda_1(y_1 + (1 + r)b - c_1 - (1 + \rho)\beta) \qquad (9.9)$$

where λ_0 and λ_1 are Lagrangian multipliers. Then the conditions for maximization are:

$$c_0 \geqslant 0, \ u_0 - \lambda_0 = 0 \qquad (9.10)$$

$$c_1 \geqslant 0, \ u_1 - \lambda_1 = 0 \qquad (9.11)$$

$$b \geqslant 0, \ [-\lambda_0 + \lambda_1(1 + r)] \geqslant 0 \qquad (9.12)$$

$$\beta \geqslant 0, \ [\lambda_0 - \lambda_1(1 + \rho)] \geqslant 0 \qquad (9.13)$$

$$[-\lambda_0 + \lambda_1(1 + r)]b = 0 \qquad (9.14)$$

$$[\lambda_0 - \lambda_1(1 + \rho)]\beta = 0 \qquad (9.15)$$

and (9.7) and (9.8).

Note that if b and β were both positive, then (9.14) and (9.15) would imply that:

$$-\lambda_0 + \lambda_1(1 + r) = \lambda_0 - \lambda_1(1 + \rho) = 0$$

which is impossible when, by assumption $\rho > r$. Hence, the model has the (unsurprising) implication that the individual will not be simultaneously both a borrower and a lender.

Notes: Chapter 9

1   This is true even of techniques for comparing the welfare of individuals facing different consumption sets, such as King's conception of

'equivalent income'. This requires for its implementation the assumption of a common functional form across individuals and, in the case of non-linear budget constraints, sufficient information concerning preferences to calculate 'virtual' prices as well. See M. King (1983b), esp. pp. 188–9.

2   There are several other contributions (cited by Sen 1985, p. 60) concerning the problem of 'set-evaluation' under uncertainty. However, the approach they use is unsuitable either for Sen's purposes or for ours. For example, under certain circumstances, adding another element to the set – seen as inferior by the individual concerned – would make the set worse. 'For choice under uncertainty, this is indeed reasonable, since the person might quite possibly end up with the inferior alternative in the enhanced set. If, however, the intention is to assess the opportunities that a person has, then adding an inferior alternative need not make the position any worse' (Sen 1985, p. 60).

3   The difficulties involved in measuring life-time income when capital markets are imperfect through the use of present discounted value measures has been discussed by Layard and others (see Layard 1977, and Layard and Zabalza 1979 and Creedy 1990). On the assumption that the appropriate procedure is to use a common discount rate, Layard offers several arguments as to why, in practice, it would be preferable to use lower rates. However, although for many practical purposes some such procedure may be essential, it does not meet our properties. For instance, the use of a common discount rate could yield the same measure of income for individuals who actually face quite different borrowing and lending interest rates and, hence, different choice sets; thus the HE property is violated.

Creedy based his analysis on an earlier (but not materially different) version of the model used here. He examined the implications of adding a borrowing limit and of using iso-elastic utility functions. He provided numerical illustrations showing that, if utility functions are iso-elastic, the use of present values, in the presence of capital market imperfections will not be too misleading, so long as interest rates are low and individuals are not affected by a borrowing constraint. Although this is clearly important for many practical purposes, it does not resolve the theoretical problem posed in the chapter, and hence cannot serve as the basis for a general resolution of these problems.

4   The formula gives the correct expression for life-time wealth (as defined by Pissarides) for individual A; but note that it not only places him on the same indifference curve but at the same point.

The error seems to have arisen because Pissarides, in calculating Y, assumes that the ratio of the shadow prices of the constraints (λ_1, λ_0 in our model) has to be the same as in the original optimization process. In fact, there is no such necessity; indeed, in general, they will not be the same.

5   One possibility that does not violate the HE property is the constant

level of consumption that could be sustained over two periods: the point where the budget constraint cuts the 45° line. However, this would fail to meet the VE property; for changes in the interest rates applicable to the sections of the budget line not cut by the 45° line would leave the measure unaffected.

6 Strictly, the existence of unearned income is not a source of non-linearity in the budget constraint; rather, it is a shift parameter. However, it creates exactly the same problems as the more conventional forms of non-linearity discussed in the text.

10 Afterword

While I would not claim for equity what Rawls claimed for justice (that it is the 'first virtue of social institutions'; see above, p. 18), it is a value whose social significance is unquestionable. That policies should be equitable, that the distributional consequences of policies should, so far as possible, be just or fair; these are considerations that policy-makers ignore at their peril. A society that most of its members consider to be governed unjustly is an unstable one; indeed, a widespread feeling of social injustice is one of the most potent factors in revolutions.

Yet considerations of equity have not always been adequately incorporated into policy formulation. This is perhaps partly because it has not always had the salience for policy-makers themselves that it has for the bulk of the people whom the policies affect. But it also arises because of a lack of an agreed definition as to what equity actually means; a fact that, as we saw in Chapter 2, has led some writers to despair of ever finding an interpretation that would command general consensus.

This book has been an attempt to counter that despair. It is true that many conceptions of equity (especially, but not exclusively, those developed by economists) do not seem to capture the essence of the term as it is conventionally used; and, that being the case, it is unlikely that any of them will command a wide measure of agreement. However, there is one common factor that does seem to underlie most judgements about the equity or otherwise of specific situations. This concerns the range of choices open to the individuals involved. Situations where one person is disadvantaged relative to another due to factors beyond either's control are commonly judged inequitable; situations where the disadvantage arises because of differences in individual choices freely made are not. Equity depends on the extent of individual choice.

In much of the book I have been concerned with the development of this idea and with addressing some of the philosophical objections to it. But the aim of the book has not only been to provide one possible resolution of a philosophical argument. It has also tried to show how the essential idea can be used in the formulation and analysis of policy. Thus the idea, and the conceptions of equity derived from it, have been applied to areas as diverse as health policy, intergovernmental grants and the measurement of income for tax purposes. Although in all these areas much remains to be done, I hope that enough has been said to show that equity, interpreted in this way, can be usefully incorporated into policy.

A final reflection concerns equity and economics. Equity considerations have often sat rather uneasily within the discipline. Although much of the literature on welfare economics currently brackets equity with efficiency as one of the two principal aims of policy, it is almost invariably efficiency that receives the lion's share of the analytic attention. However, the analysis of equity presents as exciting a challenge as the analysis of efficiency – perhaps even a greater one, given the primitive state of equity analysis. If the arguments here only serve to stimulate others to respond to that challenge, the book will have served a useful purpose.

References

Abell, P. 1989. An equitarian market socialism. In J. Le Grand and S. Estrin (eds), *Market Socialism*. Oxford: Oxford University Press.

Ackerman, B. 1980. *Social Justice in the Liberal State*. New Haven, Conn.: Yale University Press.

Adams, J. 1963. Towards an understanding of inequity. *Journal of Abnormal and Social Psychology*, vol. 67, no. 5, pp. 422–36.

Adams, J. 1965. Inequity in social exchange. In L. Berkowitz (ed.), *Advances in Experimental Social Psychology*, Vol. 2. New York: Academic Press.

Ahmad, E. and Stern, N. 1984. The theory of reform and Indian indirect taxes. *Journal of Public Economics*, vol. 25, no. 3, pp. 259–98.

Alves, W. and Rossi, P. 1978. Who should get what? Fairness judgments of the distribution of earnings. *American Journal of Sociology*, vol. 84, no. 3, pp. 541–64.

Archibald, G. and Donaldson, D. 1979. Notes on economic equality. *Journal of Public Economics*, vol. 12, no. 2, pp. 205–14.

Arneson, R. 1989. Equality and equality of opportunity for welfare. *Philosophical Studies*, vol. 56, no. 1, pp. 77–93.

Aronson, J. 1977. Some comments on fiscal equity and grants to local authorities. *Economic Journal*, vol. 87, no. 348, pp. 774–9.

Arrow, K. 1973. Some ordinalist-utilitarian notes on Rawls' theory of justice. *Journal of Philosophy*, vol. 70, no. 9, pp. 245–63.

Atkinson, A. B. 1970. On the measurement of inequality. *Journal of Economic Theory*, vol. 2, no. 3, pp. 244–63.

Atkinson, A. B. 1980. Horizontal equity and the distribution of the tax burden. In H. Aaron and M. Boskin (eds), *The Economics of Taxation*. Washington, DC: Brookings Institution.

Atkinson, A. B. 1983a. The commitment to equality. In J. Griffith (ed.), *Socialism in a Cold Climate*. London: Allen and Unwin.

Atkinson, A. B. 1983b. *The Economics of Inequality*. Oxford: Oxford University Press.

Atkinson, A. B. 1983c. *Social Justice and Public Policy*. Brighton: Harvester–Wheatsheaf.

Atkinson, A. B. and Stiglitz, J. 1980. *Lectures in Public Economics*. New York: McGraw-Hill.

Barr, N. 1987. *The Economics of the Welfare State*. London: Weidenfeld and Nicolson.

Barry, B. 1965. *Political Argument*. London: Routledge and Kegan Paul.

Barry, B. 1973. *The Liberal Theory of Justice*. Oxford: Clarendon Press.

Barry, B. 1989a. *Democracy, Power and Justice*. Oxford: Oxford University Press.

Barry, B. 1989b. *Theories of Justice*. Berkeley and Los Angeles, Calif.: University of California Press.

Barry, B. 1990. Choice, chance and justice. Expanded text of a Public Lecture, London School of Economics, 25 April 1990. (Forthcoming in revised edition of Barry 1989a.)

Basu, K. 1980. *Revealed Preferences of Government*. Cambridge: Cambridge University Press.

Bauer, P. 1982. *Equality, the Third World and Economic Delusion*. London: Methuen.

Bauer, P. 1983. The grail of equality. In W. Letwin (ed.), 1983.

Baumol, W. 1986. *Superfairness: Applications and Theory*. Cambridge, Mass: MIT Press.

Bellah, R., Madsen, R., Sullivan, W., Swidler, A. and Tipton, S. 1988. *Habits of the Heart: Middle America Observed*. London: Hutchinson.

Berliant, M. and Strauss, R. 1985. The horizontal and vertical equity characteristics of the federal income tax, 1966–1977. Ch. 7 in M. David and T. Smeeding (eds), *Horizontal Equity, Uncertainty and Economic Well-Being*, pp. 179–211. Chicago: University of Chicago Press.

Black, D. 1980. *Inequalities in Health*. Report of a research working group chaired by Sir Douglas Black. London: Department of Health and Social Security.

Boyle, L. 1966. *Equalisation and the Future of Local Government Finance*. Edinburgh: Oliver and Boyd.

Bradford, F. and Oates, W. 1971. An analysis of revenue sharing. *Quarterly Journal of Economics*, vol. 85, no. 3, pp. 416–39.

Bramley, G. 1990. *Equalization Grants and Local Expenditure Needs*. Aldershot: Avebury.

Broome, J. 1989. Economic analysis and ethics. Discussion Paper No. 89/242. University of Bristol: Department of Economics. Forthcoming in L. Becker and C. Becker (eds), *Encyclopedia of Ethics*. New York: Garland Publishing.

Broome, J. (forthcoming). *Weighing Goods*. Oxford: Blackwell.

Browning, E. K. and Johnson, W. R. 1984. The trade-off between equality and efficiency. *Journal of Political Economy*, vol. 92, no. 2, pp. 175–203.

Buchanan, J. 1950. Federalism and fiscal equity. *American Economic Review*, vol. 40, no. 4, pp. 583–99.

Buchanan, J. 1952. Federal grants and resource allocation. *Journal of Political Economy*, vol. 60, no. 3, pp. 208–17.

Christiansen, V. and Jansen, E. 1978. Implicit social preferences in the Norwegian system of indirect taxation. *Journal of Public Economics*, vol. 10, no. 2, pp. 217–45.

Cohen, G. 1989. On the currency of egalitarian justice. *Ethics*, vol. 99, July, pp. 906–44.

Collard, D. 1978. *Altruism and Economy*. Oxford: Martin Robertson.

Cowell, F. 1979. The definition of lifetime income. Discussion Paper No. 566-79. Madison, Wis.: Institute for Research on Poverty.

Creedy, J. 1990. Measuring wealth in a simple two-period model. *Journal of Econometrics*, vol. 43, pp. 167–77.

Culyer, A. J. 1988. Inequality in health services is, in general, desirable. In D. Green (ed.) (1988) pp. 31–47.

Daniels, N. (ed.) 1975. *Reading Rawls*. Oxford: Blackwell.

Daniels, N. 1985. *Just Health Care*. Cambridge: Cambridge University Press.

Dasgupta, A. and Pearce, D. 1978. *Cost-Benefit Analysis: Theory and Practice*. London: Macmillan.

Dasgupta, P. 1982. Utilitarianism, information and rights. In A. Sen and B. Williams (eds.), *Utilitarianism and Beyond*. Cambridge: Cambridge University Press.

Dasgupta, P. 1989. Positive freedom, markets and the welfare state. In D. Helm (ed.), *The Economic Borders of the State*. Oxford: Oxford University Press, pp. 110–26.

Dasgupta, P., Marglin, S. and Sen, A. 1972. *Guidelines for Project Evaluation*. United Nations Industrial Development Organization, Project Formulation and Evaluation Series, No. 2. New York: United Nations.

Deutsch, M. 1985. *Distributive Justice*. New Haven, Conn.: Yale University Press.

Dickinson, H. 1953. Some observations on the marginal utility of income and on the equitable tax. *Economia Internazionale*, vol. 6, pp. 342–52.

Doyal, L. and Gough, I. 1984. A theory of human needs. *Critical Social Policy*, vol. 4, no. 1, pp. 4–38.

Drèze, J. and Stern, N. 1985. The theory of cost-benefit analysis. Discussion Paper No. 59. Coventry: Development Economics Research Centre, University of Warwick.

Dubins, L. E. and Spanier, E. H. 1961. How to cut a cake fairly. *American Mathematical Monthly*, vol. 68, pp. 1–17.

Dworkin, R. 1981a. What is equality? Part 1: Equality of welfare. *Philosophy and Public Affairs*, vol. 10, no. 3, pp. 185–247.

Dworkin, R. 1981b. What is equality? Part 2: Equality of resources. *Philosophy and Public Affairs*, vol. 10, no. 4, pp. 283–345.

Eckstein, O. 1961. A survey of the theory of public expenditure criteria. In Conference of the Universities–National Bureau for Economic Research. *Public Finances: Needs, Sources and Utilization*. Princeton, NJ: Princeton University Press.

Feinberg, J. 1975. Rawls and intuitionism. In N. Daniels (ed.), 1975, pp. 108–124.

Feldstein, M. S. 1976. On the theory of tax reform. *Journal of Public Economics*, vol. 6, nos 1–2, pp. 77–104.

Foley, D. 1967. Resource allocation and the public sector. *Yale Economic Essays*, vol. 7, no. 1, pp. 45–98.

Foster, C., Jackman, R. and Perlman, M. 1980. *Local Government Finance in a Unitary State*. London: Allen and Unwin.

Friedman, M. 1962. *Capitalism and Freedom*. Chicago: University of Chicago Press.

Giertz, J. 1982. A limited defense of Pareto optimal redistribution. *Public Choice*, vol. 39, no. 2, pp. 277–82.

Glover, J. 1977. *Causing Death and Saving Lives*. Harmondsworth: Penguin.

Godley, W. and Rhodes, J. 1973. The rate support grant system. Published in the Proceedings of a Conference on Local Government Finance, December. London Institute of Fiscal Studies.

Golding, P. and Middleton, S. 1982. *Images of Welfare*. Oxford: Oxford University Press.

Goodin, R. 1985. *Protecting the Vulnerable: A Reanalysis of our Social Responsibilities*. Chicago: University of Chicago Press.

Goodin, R. 1988. *Reasons for Welfare: The Political Theory of the Welfare State*. Princeton, NJ: Princeton University Press.

Goodin, R. and Wilenski, P. 1984. Beyond efficiency: the logical under-pinnings of administrative principle, *Public Administration Review*, vol. 44, no. 6, pp. 512–17.

Gordon, R. 1976. Essays on the causes and equitable treatment of differences in earnings and abilities. Unpublished PhD thesis, Cambridge, Mass: MIT.

Gray, J. 1984. *Hayek on Liberty*. Oxford: Blackwell.

Green, D. (ed.) 1988. *Acceptable Inequalities? Essays on the pursuit of equality in health care*. IEA Health Unit Paper No. 3. London: The Institute of Economic Affairs Health Unit.

Grossman, M. 1972. *The Demand for Health*. New York: Columbia University Press.

Habermas, J. 1976. *Legitimation Crisis*. London: Heinemann.

Hammond, P. J. 1976. Equity, Arrow's conditions and Rawls' difference principle. *Econometrica*, vol. 44, no. 4, pp. 793–804.

Hammond, P. J. 1977. Dual interpersonal comparisons of utility and the welfare economics of income distribution. *Journal of Public Economics*, vol. 7, no. 1, pp. 51–71.

Hare, R. M. 1981. *Moral Thinking*. Oxford: Clarendon Press.

Harsanyi, J. 1955. Cardinal welfare, individualistic ethics and interpersonal comparisons of utility. *Journal of Political Economy*, vol. 63, no. 4, pp. 309–21.

Haveman, R. H. 1965. *Water Resource Investment and the Public Interest*. Nashville, Tenn.: Vanderbilt University Press.

Hayek, F. A. 1978. *The Mirage of Social Justice: Law, Legislation and Liberty*, Vol. 2. London: Routledge and Kegan Paul.

Hicks, J. R. 1940–1. The rehabilitation of consumer surplus. *The Review of Economic Studies*, vol. 8, no. 2, pp. 108–16.

Hicks, J. R. and Hicks, U. 1943. *The Incidence of Local Rates in Great Britain: The Problem of Valuation for Rating; Standards of Local Expenditure*. Cambridge: Cambridge University Press.

Hochman, H. and Rodgers, J. 1969. Pareto-optimal redistribution. *American Economic Review*, vol. 59, no. 4, pp. 542–57.

Hochschild, J. 1981. *What's Fair? American Beliefs about Distributive Justice*. Cambridge, Mass: Harvard University Press.

Homans, G. 1961. *Social Behaviour: Its Elementary Forms*. New York: Harcourt Brace and World.

Hoover, K. and Plant, R. 1989. *Conservative Capitalism in Britain and the United States*. London: Routledge and Kegan Paul.

Jenkins, S. 1988. Empirical measurement of horizontal inequity. *Journal of Public Economics*, vol. 37, no. 3, pp. 305–29.

Joseph, K. and Sumption, J. 1979. *Equality*. London: John Murray.

Jowell, R., Witherspoon, S. and Brook, L. 1988. *British Social Attitudes: the Fifth Report*. Aldershot: Gower.

King, D. 1984. *Fiscal Tiers: The Economics of Multi-Level Government*. London: Allen and Unwin.

King, M. 1983a. An index of inequality; with applications to horizontal equity and social mobility. *Econometrica*, vol. 51, no. 1, pp. 99–115.

King, M. 1983b. Welfare analysis of tax reforms using household data. *Journal of Public Economics*, vol. 21, no. 2, pp. 183–214.

Klein, R. 1988. Acceptable inequalities. In D. Green (ed.), 1988, pp. 1–20.

Kluegel, J. and Smith, E. 1986. *Beliefs About Inequality: American Views of What Is and What Ought to Be*. New York: Aldine de Gruyter.

Kolm, S-C. 1972. *Justice et Equité*. Paris: Editions de Centre National de la Recherche Scientifique.

Layard, R. 1977. On measuring the redistribution of life-time income. In M. Feldstein and R. Inman (eds), *The Economics of Public Services*. London: Macmillan.

Layard, R. and Walters, R. 1978. *Microeconomic Theory*. Maidenhead: McGraw-Hill.

Layard, R. and Zabalza, A. 1979. Family income distribution: explanation and policy evaluation. *Journal of Political Economy*, vol. 87, no. 5, part 2, pp. S133–S161.

Le Grand, J. 1975a. Fiscal equity and central government grants to local authorities. *Economic Journal*, vol. 85, no. 339, pp. 531–47.

Le Grand, J. 1975b. Public price discrimination and aid to low income groups. *Economica*, vol. 42, pp. 32–42.

Le Grand, J. 1977. Reply. *Economic Journal*, vol. 87, no. 348, pp. 780–2.

Le Grand, J. 1982. *The Strategy of Equality*. London: Allen and Unwin.

Le Grand, J. 1984a. Equity as an economic objective. *Journal of Applied Philosophy*, vol. 1, no. 1, pp. 39–51.

Le Grand, J. 1984b. Optimal taxation, the compensation principle and the measurement of changes in economic welfare. *Journal of Public Economics*, vol. 24, no. 2, pp. 241–7.

Le Grand, J. 1987. Equity, health and health care. *Social Justice Research*, vol. 1, no. 3, pp. 257–74.

Le Grand, J. 1988. Equity, well-being and economic choice. *Journal of Human Resources*, vol. 22, no. 3, pp. 429–40.

Le Grand, J. 1990. Equity vs efficiency: the elusive trade-off. *Ethics*, vol. 10, no. 3, pp. 554–68.

Le Grand, J. and Reschovsky, A. 1971. Concerning the appropriate formulae for achieving horizontal equity through federal revenue sharing. *National Tax Journal*, vol. 24, no. 4, pp. 475–86.

Le Grand, J., Propper, C. and Robinson, R. 1991. *The Economics of Social Problems*. London: Macmillan.

Letwin, W. (ed.) 1983. *Against Equality*. London: Macmillan.

McClosky, H. and Zaller, J. 1984. *The American Ethos: Public Attitudes towards Capitalism and Democracy*. Cambridge, Mass: Harvard University Press.

McLachlan, G. and Maynard, A. K. (eds) 1982. *The Public/Private Mix for Health*. London: The National Provincial Hospitals Trust.

Marshall, G. 1990. Does social order require social justice? Paper presented to the International Justice Project, Utrecht, 27–30.

Marshall, G., Newby, H., Rose, D. and Vogler, C. 1988. *Social Class in Modern Britain*. London: Unwin Hyman.

Maynard, A. and Williams, A. 1984. Privatisation and the National Health Service. In J. Le Grand and R. Robinson (eds), *Privatisation and the Welfare State*. London: Allen and Unwin.

Mera, K. 1969. Experimental determination of relative marginal utilities. *Quarterly Journal of Economics*, vol. 83, no. 3, pp. 464–77.

Miller, D. 1976. *Social Justice*. Oxford: Oxford University Press.

Mishan, E. J. 1976. *Cost-Benefit Analysis*. New York: Praeger.

Mooney, G. 1986. *Economics, Medicine and Health Care*. Brighton: Wheatsheaf.

Musgrave, R. A. 1959. *The Theory of Public Finance*. New York: McGraw-Hill.

Musgrave, R. A. 1961. Approaches to a fiscal theory of political federalism. In *Public Finance: Needs, Sources and Utilization*. Princeton, NJ: Princeton University Press.

Musgrave, R. A. 1976. ET, OT and SBT. *Journal of Public Economics*, vol. 6, no. 1, pp. 3–16.

Ng, Y. K. 1972. Value judgements and economists' role in policy recommendations. *Economic Journal*, vol. 82, no. 327, pp. 1014–18.

Nowick, R. 1974. *Anarchy, State and Utopia*. New York: Basic Books.

Oates, W. 1982. *Fiscal Federalism*. New York: Harcourt Brace Jovanovich.

Okun, A. 1975. *Equality and Efficiency: The Big Trade-off*. Washington, DC: Brookings.

Olsen, E. and Rogers, D. (forthcoming). The welfare economics of equal access. *Journal of Public Economics*.

Pasour, E. 1981. Pareto optimality as a guide to income redistribution. *Public Choice*, vol. 36, no. 1, pp. 75–87.

Pasour, E. 1983. A limited defense of Pareto optimal redistribution: Comment. *Public Choice*, vol. 41, no. 3, pp. 451–4.

Pazner, E. 1975. Pitfalls in the theory of fairness. *Journal of Economic Theory*, vol. 14, no. 2, pp. 458–66.

Pazner, E. and Schmeidler, D. 1974. A difficulty in the concept of fairness. *Review of Economic Studies*, vol. 41, pp. 441–3.

Pazner, E. and Schmeidler, D. 1978. Egalitarian-equivalent allocations: a new concept of economic equity. *Quarterly Journal of Economics*, vol. 92, no. 4, pp. 1–45.

Pereira, J. 1989. What does equity in health care mean? Discussion Paper no. 61. York: Centre for Health Economics, University of York.

Pettit, P. 1980. *Judging Justice: An Introduction to Contemporary Political Philosophy*. London: Routledge and Kegan Paul.

Pissarides, C. 1978. Liquidity considerations in the theory of consumption. *Quarterly Journal of Economics*, vol. 92, no. 2, pp. 279–96.

Plant, R. 1984. *Equality, Markets and the State*. Fabian Tract No. 494. London: Fabian Society.

Plant, R., Lesser, H. and Taylor-Gooby, P. 1980. *Political Philosophy and Social Welfare: Essays on the Normative Basis of Welfare Provision*. London: Routledge and Kegan Paul.

Plotnick, R. 1981. A measure of horizontal inequity. *Review of Economics and Statistics*, vol. 63, no. 2, pp. 283–8.

Plotnick, R. 1982. The concept and measurement of horizontal inequity. *Journal of Public Economics*, vol. 17, no. 3, pp. 373–91.

Plotnick, R. 1985. A comparison of measures of horizontal inequity. In M. David and T. Smeeding (eds), *Horizontal Equity, Uncertainty and Economic Well-being*, pp. 239–68. Chicago: University of Chicago Press.

Preinreich, G. 1948. Progressive taxation and sacrifice. *American Economic Review*, vol. 38, no. 1, pp. 103–17.

Rawls, J. 1972. *A Theory of Justice*. Oxford: Oxford University Press.

Rawls, J. 1974. Some reasons for the maximin criterion. *American Economic Review*, vol. 64, no. 2 (Proc.), pp. 141–6.

Rees, J. 1971. *Equality*. London: Pall Mall Press.

Roemer, J. 1986. Equality of resources implies equality of welfare. *Quarterly Journal of Economics*, vol. 101, no. 4, pp. 751–84.

Robinson, R. and Bell, W. 1978. Equality, success and social justice in England and the United States. *American Sociological Review*, vol. 43, no. 2, pp. 125–43.

Sampson, E. 1969. Studies in status congruence. In L. Berkowitz and E. Walster (eds), *Advances in Experimental Social Psychology*, Vol. 4, pp. 225–70. New York: Academic Press.

Scafuri, A. 1986. Measurable welfare change with optimal commodity taxation. *Journal of Public Economics*, vol. 29, no. 3, pp. 383–7.

Schlozman, K. and Verba, S. 1979. *Injury to Insult: Unemployment, Class and Political Response*. Cambridge, Mass: Harvard University Press.

Sen, A. 1973. *On Economic Inequality*. Oxford: Oxford University Press.

Sen, A. 1980. Equality of what? In S. McMurrin (ed.), *The Tanner Lectures in Human Values*, Vol. 1. Salt Lake City, Utah: University of Utah Press.

Sen, A. 1982. *Choice, Welfare and Measurement*. Oxford: Blackwell.

Sen, A. 1985. *Commodities and Capabilities*. Professor Dr P. Hennipman Lectures in Economics 7. Amsterdam: North Holland.

Sidgwick, H. 1907. *The Methods of Ethics*, 7th edn. London: Macmillan.

Soltan, K. 1982. Empirical studies of distributive justice. *Ethics*, vol. 92, no. 4, pp. 673–91.

Stern, N. 1977. Welfare weights and the elasticity of the marginal valuation of income. In M. Artis and A. R. Nobay (eds), *Studies in Modern Economic Analysis*, pp. 209–54. Oxford: Blackwell.

Stolte, J. 1987. The formation of justice norms. *American Sociological Review*, vol. 52, no. 6, pp. 774–84.

Sugden, R. 1984. Is fairness good? A critique of Varian's theory of fairness. *Noûs*, vol. 18, no. 3, pp. 505–11.

Sugden, R. 1986. *The Economics of Rights, Co-operation and Welfare*. Oxford: Blackwell.

Sugden, R. and Weale, A. 1979. A contractual reformulation of certain aspects of welfare economics. *Economica*, vol. 46, pp. 111–23.

Taussig, M. 1973. *Alternative Measures of the Distribution of Economic Welfare*. Princeton, NJ: Princeton University Industrial Relation Section.

Tawney, R. H. 1964. *Equality*. Fifth edition. London: Unwin Books. First published in 1931.

Taylor-Gooby, P. 1985. *Public Opinion, Ideology and State Welfare*. London: Routledge and Kegan Paul.

Thurow, L. 1970. Aid to state and local governments. *National Tax Journal*, vol. 33, no. 1, pp. 23–55.

Tobin, J. 1970. On limiting the domain of inequality. *Journal of Law and Economics*, vol. 13, no. 2, pp. 263–77.

Törnblom, K. and Foa, U. 1983. Choice of a distribution principle: cross-cultural evidence on the effects of resources. *Acta Sociologica*, vol. 26, no. 2, pp. 161–73.

Törnblom, K., Jonsson, D. and Knowles, E. 1982. When justice is and is not requested: the effects of non-recipient allocators' social awareness and recipient categorization on the choice of distribution rule. Paper presented at the Ninetieth Annual Convention of the American Psychological Association, Washington, DC.

Tullock, G. 1983. *The Economics of Income Redistribution*. Boston: Kluwer-Nijhoff.

United Kingdom Treasury. 1990. *The Government's Public Expenditure Plans* 1990–91 to 1992–93. London: HMSO.

Varian, H. 1974. Equity, envy and efficiency. *Journal of Economic Theory*, vol. 9, no. 1, pp. 63–91.

Varian, H. 1975. Distributive justice, welfare economics and the theory of fairness. *Philosophy and Public Affairs*, vol. 4, no. 3, pp. 223–47.

Varian, H. 1984. *Microeconomic Analysis*, 2nd edn. New York: W. W. Norton.

von Wright, G. 1963. *The Varieties of Goodness*. London: Routledge and Kegan Paul.

Walzer, M. 1983. *Spheres of Justice*. New York: Basic Books.

Weale, A. 1978. *Equality and Social Policy*. London: Routledge and Kegan Paul.

Weale, A. 1983. *Political Theory and Social Policy*. London: Macmillan.

Webb, S. 1920. *Grants in Aid*. London: Longman.

Webster, M. and Smith, L. 1978. Justice and revolutionary coalitions: a test of two theories. *American Journal of Sociology*, vol. 84, no. 2, pp. 267–92.

Weisbrod, B. 1968. Income redistribution effects and benefit-cost analysis.

In S. Chase (ed.), *Problems in Public Expenditure Analysis*. Washington, DC: Brookings.

Williams, A. 1978. Need – an economic exegesis. In A. J. Culyer and K. G. Wright (eds), *Economic Aspects of Health Services*. London: Martin Robertson.

Williams, B. 1962. The idea of equality. In P. Laslett and W. Runciman (eds), *Philosophy, Politics and Society*. Series 2. Oxford: Blackwell.

Wolff, R. P. 1972. *Understanding Rawls*. Princeton, NJ: Princeton University Press.

Index